Rawlicious Desserts

From Fragrant Vanilla Cake

A few words from Amy:

Hi, I am Amy the blogger and recipe developer behind the blog Fragrant Vanilla Cake! My passion is developing delicious recipes to share and allow you to experience food the way that I do in my own kitchen. This book is a compilation of my favorite raw dessert recipes. I am fairly new to raw food, but I would like to share with you the knowledge I have gained over the past year. The recipes in this book are raw, so no ovens or forms of cooking the food above 115 degrees F are used. They may require special equipment such as a dehydrator or a high speed blender but those items are well worth it, if you are serious about the raw food lifestyle. If you are new to raw, there are also recipes which are simpler and only require refrigeration or freezing to set them. There is a little something for everyone in this book, and I hope you enjoy making the recipes as much as I do. It is my goal to inspire others to try eating more raw and healthful foods

Recipe Index

Cakes and Cheesecakes

Cake, especially cheesecake, is my favorite type of dessert, which is why in this chapter you will find that there are the most of these recipes. I start off the chapter with my most popular cake recipe, Raw Blackberry Lemon Lavender Cheesecake. You will find all sorts of flavors here though, everything from carrot cake to red velvet doughnuts! If you enjoy chocolate and spice, there is even a Mexican Chocolate Turtle Cheesecake!

Raw Blackberry Lemon Lavender Cheesecake

Makes one 6 inch cake

Six inch spring form pan

Crust:
2/3 cup hazelnuts
2/3 cup finely shredded coconut
1/3 cup sprouted, dehydrated buckwheat groats (or additional coconut)
1/8 teaspoon sea salt
3 soft medjool dates, pitted and chopped

Filling:
2 1/2 cups raw cashews (soaked at least 4 hours, but preferably soaked overnight)
1 cup young coconut meat (or additional soaked cashews)
1/2 cup lemon juice
2 Tbsp lemon zest
1/3 cup plus 3 Tbsp raw coconut nectar or agave nectar
1/2 teaspoon sea salt
1 Tbsp pure vanilla extract and seeds from half a vanilla bean (other half reserved for topping)
1/2 cup plus 1 Tbsp coconut oil (warmed to liquid)
2 Tbsp organic dried lavender flowers

1 cup fresh organic blackberries

Blackberry puree:
1/4 cup organic blackberries
1 Tbsp organic coconut nectar or agave nectar

Cream Topping:
3/4 cup raw cashew pieces (soaked at least 4 hours, but preferably soaked overnight)
1/4 cup coconut water
1 cup fresh young coconut meat* (or additional soaked cashews if not available)
3 Tbsp raw coconut nectar or agave syrup
1 teaspoon vanilla and seeds of half a vanilla bean (the other half of the one you

used for the filling)
1/4 cup raw coconut oil (warmed to liquid)

To prepare the crust, spray a 6 inch spring form pan with coconut oil spray or grease with coconut oil. Process hazelnuts, coconut, buckwheat and sea salt in a food processor until they are fine crumbs, then add the dates and process until the mixture holds together when squeezed between your fingers. Firmly press crust into the bottom of prepared pan. Set aside.

To make filling, drain cashews and combine them with lemon juice, and zest, agave nectar, sea salt, and vanilla in a food processor and blend until smooth and creamy. With the motor running, slowly add the coconut oil in a thin stream to emulsify (if you get small chunks the mixture was too cold or the coconut oil was too cold, and if this happens, remove a small portion of the filling, warm it slightly and return it to the bowl. It should emulsify). Remove the filling from the food processor, stir in lavender and divide evenly between 2 bowls. Place half back into the food processor and add 1 cup blackberries. Puree until smooth and scrape back in the bowl. For the blackberry puree, using an immersion blender (or you can rinse out the food processor) combine the 1/4 cup blackberries and 1 Tbsp agave nectar and puree until smooth. Drop the filling alternating between the vanilla and blackberry in about 3 tablespoonful amounts over crust in pan, until all is used up, sort of in a checkerboard fashion. Tap on the countertop to level (keeping pan level). Drop some of the puree in teaspoonful amounts over the top of the cake (reserving some for serving) and swirl with a knife to create marbling. Place in the freezer until it is set, about 6 hours. After that, store in the fridge until ready to top.

To make topping, drain cashews and blend all ingredients until smooth in a food processor, and set in the freezer about 30 minutes until a frosting consistency. Place in a pastry bag and pipe decoratively on top of the cheesecake. Store in the refrigerator when not enjoying.

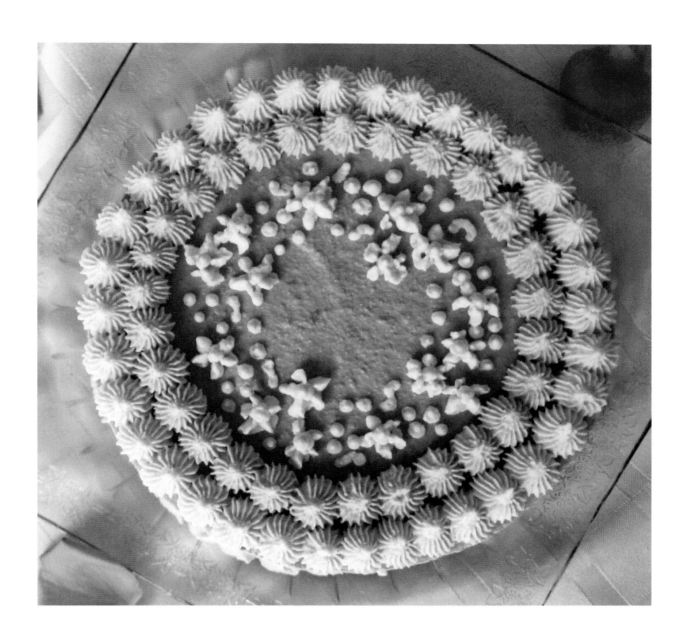

Raw Pretty in Pink Birthday Cheesecake

Makes one 6 inch cake

Crust:
3/4 cup shelled pistachios
1/8 teaspoon sea salt
3-4 soft medjool dates, pitted and chopped

Filling:
2 1/2 cups raw cashews (preferably soaked overnight and drained)
1/2 cup young coconut meat (or additional soaked cashews)
1/2 cup coconut water (or filtered water)
1 tsp rosewater
1 Tbsp lemon juice
1/3 cup plus 3 Tbsp agave nectar or honey
1/2 cup plus 1 Tbsp coconut oil (warmed to liquid)
1/2 teaspoon sea salt
1 Tbsp pure vanilla extract and seeds from half a vanilla bean (other half reserved for topping)
1/2 cup fresh organic strawberries
1/2 cup fresh organic red raspberries
1 Tbsp organic lavender

Cream Topping:
3/4 cup raw cashew pieces (preferably soaked overnight)
1/2 cup coconut water
3/4 cup fresh young coconut meat (or additional soaked cashews if not available)
2 tablespoons agave nectar or honey
1 teaspoon pure vanilla extract and seeds of half a vanilla bean (reserved from filling)
1/4 cup coconut oil (warmed to liquid)

4-6 fresh organic raspberries

Lightly coat a 6 inch spring form removable bottom pan with coconut oil. To prepare the crust, process pistachios and sea salt in a food processor until the pistachios are fine crumbs, and then add the dates and process until the mixture holds together when squeezed between your fingers. Firmly press crust into the bottom of the prepared pan, and set aside.

To make the filling, drain the cashews and combine them with coconut meat, coconut water, lemon juice, rosewater, agave nectar, coconut oil, sea salt and vanilla in a food processor and blend until smooth and creamy. Remove the filling from the food processor, and divide evenly between 3 bowls. Place 1/3 into the food processor and add 1/2 cup of strawberries. Puree until smooth and scrape back in the bowl. Add another 1/3 of the filling to the food processor and add 1/2 cup raspberries, and puree until smooth. Add the lavender to the third bowl and stir in until combined.

To assemble the cheesecake, pour the vanilla lavender filling over the crust, then smooth to the sides. Then pour the strawberry filling and lastly the raspberry filling. Place cheesecake in the freezer until it is set (4 to 6 hours), then once set, store in the refrigerator.

To make topping, drain cashews and blend all ingredients until smooth in a food processor, then divide into 2 bowls. Place one half back in the food processor and throw in about 4-6 raspberries, and blend (to tint pink). Place back in the bowl, and set bowls in the freezer about 30 minutes until a frosting consistency. Place the two frostings in pastry bags and pipe decoratively around the top and bottom of the cheesecake. Store leftover cake in the refrigerator.

Raw PB & J Swirl Cheesecake

Makes one 6 inch cheesecake

Crust:
1/2 cup raw peanuts or pecans, soaked and dried
1/2 cup sprouted buckwheat, dried in the dehydrator (or additional pecans)
1/2 cup shredded dried unsweetened coconut
1/8 teaspoon sea salt
10-12 soft medjool dates, pitted and chopped

Filling:
2 cups young coconut meat (or if unavailable 2 cups soaked cashews, drained)
3/4 cup raw cashews (soaked at least 4 hours and drained)
3/4 cup raw peanuts (soaked at least 4 hours and drained)
1/2 cup coconut water (or filtered water)
1/2 cup raw coconut nectar or agave nectar or raw honey
1/2 cup plus 1 Tbsp raw coconut oil (warmed to liquid)
1/2 tsp sea salt
1 Tbsp pure vanilla extract and seeds from half a vanilla bean (other half reserved for topping)
1/2 cup fresh organic raspberries (or frozen and thawed, drained well)

Swirl:
1/4 cup fresh organic raspberries (or frozen and thawed, drained well)
1 Tbsp raw coconut nectar or raw agave nectar or raw honey

1/3 cup raw peanut butter
1 Tbsp raw coconut nectar or raw agave nectar

Lightly coat a 6 inch spring form removable bottom pan with coconut oil. To prepare the crust, process peanuts, buckwheat, and sea salt in a food processor until they are fine crumbs, then add the dates and process until the mixture holds together when squeezed between your fingers (if not holding together, add more dates). Firmly press crust into the bottom of the prepared pan, and set aside.

To make the filling, drain the cashews and peanuts and combine them with coconut water, coconut nectar, sea salt and vanilla in a food processor, and blend until smooth and creamy. With the processor running, add the coconut oil, and process for a minute until blended. Remove the filling from the food processor, and divide into 2 bowls. Add one back to the food processor and add 1/2 cup raspberries. Process until smooth and scrape back into the bowl.

For the raspberry swirl, puree the 1/4 cup of raspberries with 1 Tbsp coconut nectar.

For the peanut butter swirl, whisk together the 1/4 cup raw peanut butter and coconut nectar.

To assemble cheesecake, drop half the filling by the 1/2 tablespoonful over the crust randomly alternating between the peanut butter and raspberry. Drop 1/2 the raspberry puree mixture by the 1/2 teaspoonful over the filling in the pan, and do the same with the peanut butter mixture, then drop the remaining cheesecake fillings over it by the tablespoonful randomly to fill the pan. Tap lightly on the countertop to level, then drop the remaining raspberry puree and peanut butter mixture by the 1/2 teaspoonful over the top. Swirl with a knife or a thin stick, and place in the freezer for about 4-6 hours to firm up. Once set, serve! Store remaining cheesecake in the refrigerator.

Raw Piña Colada Cheesecake

Makes one 6 inch cake

Crust:
1/2 cup raw macadamia nuts
1/2 cup sprouted buckwheat, dried in the dehydrator (or additional coconut)
1/2 cup dried finely shredded coconut
1/8 teaspoon sea salt
10-12 soft medjool dates, pitted and chopped

Filling:
1 1/2 cups raw macadamia nuts or raw cashews (preferably soaked overnight and drained)
2 cups young coconut meat (or additional soaked cashews if unavailable)
1/2 cup coconut water
1/2 cup raw coconut nectar, raw agave nectar or raw honey
1/2 cup plus 2 Tbsp raw coconut oil (warmed to liquid)
1/2 teaspoon sea salt
1 Tbsp pure vanilla extract and seeds from half a vanilla bean
1 cup fresh organic pineapple

1/2 cup finely shredded coconut

Swirl:
2 medjool dates, pitted (soaked if not already soft)
1/2 cup fresh organic pineapple

Lightly coat a 6 inch spring form removable bottom pan with coconut oil. To prepare the crust, process pine nuts, buckwheat, and sea salt in a food processor until the nuts are fine crumbs, then add the dates and process until the mixture holds together when squeezed between your fingers (if not holding together, add more dates). Firmly press crust into the bottom of the prepared pan, and set aside.
To make the filling, drain the cashews and combine them with coconut, coconut water, coconut nectar, sea salt, and vanilla in a food processor, and blend until smooth and creamy. With the processor running, add the coconut oil, and process for a minute until blended. Remove the filling from the food processor and divide into 2 bowls. Place one back into the food processor and add pineapple. Process until smooth and uniform in color and place back in the bowl. Stir shredded coconut into the second bowl.
For the swirl, combine dates and pineapple in the food processor and process until smooth.
To assemble cheesecake, drop the two fillings over the crust by the tablespoonful and the pineapple swirl by the teaspoonful, until they are all used up. Tap the bottom of the pan on the countertop to level. Swirl with a knife, and place in the freezer for about 4 hours to firm up.

Raw Strawberries and Cream Dream Cake

Makes one 6 inch cake

Crust:
1/2 cup raw pine nuts
1/2 cup sprouted buckwheat, dried in the dehydrator (or additional coconut or pistachios)
1/2 cup dried finely shredded coconut
1/8 teaspoon sea salt
10-12 soft medjool dates, pitted and chopped

Filling:
1 1/2 cups raw cashews (preferably soaked overnight and drained)
2 cups young coconut meat (or additional soaked cashews if unavailable)
1/2 cup coconut water
1/2 cup raw coconut nectar, raw agave nectar or raw honey
1/2 cup plus 2 Tbsp raw coconut oil (warmed to liquid)
1/2 teaspoon sea salt
1 Tbsp pure vanilla extract and seeds from half a vanilla bean
1 1/2 cups fresh organic strawberries (divided)
1 inch piece red beet

Swirl:
1/2 cup fresh organic strawberries
1 soft medjool date, pitted

Lightly coat a 6 inch spring form removable bottom pan with coconut oil. To prepare the crust, process pine nuts, buckwheat and sea salt in a food processor until the nuts are fine crumbs, then add the dates and process, until the mixture holds together when squeezed between your fingers (if not holding together, add more dates). Firmly press crust into the bottom of the prepared pan, and set aside. To make the filling, drain the cashews and combine them with coconut, coconut water, coconut nectar, sea salt, and vanilla in a food processor, and blend until smooth and creamy. With the processor running, add the coconut oil, and process for a minute until blended. Remove the filling from the food processor and divide into 3 bowls. Place one back into the food processor and add 1/2 cup strawberries. Process until smooth and uniform in color and place back in the bowl. Add the second bowl to the food processor and 1 cup berries and the beet piece (to make the color darker than the last batch). Process until smooth and place back in the bowl. To assemble cheesecake, drop the different colors of filling over the crust by the tablespoonful and the swirl by the teaspoonful, and when they are all used up, tap the bottom of the pan on the countertop to level. Swirl with a knife starting at the outside of the circle and working your way in in a spiral fashion. Place the cheesecake in the freezer to firm up for about 4 hours until set before unmolding. Store leftover cake in the refrigerator.

Raw Mexican Dark Chocolate Turtle Cheesecake

Makes one 6 inch cake

Crust:
3/4 cup pecans, soaked and dried
3/4 cup sprouted buckwheat, dried in the dehydrator (or additional pecans)
1/8 teaspoon sea salt
10-12 soft medjool dates, pitted and chopped

Filling:
3 cups raw cashews (preferably soaked overnight and drained)
1/2 cup coconut water (or filtered water)
1/2 cup raw agave nectar or honey
1/2 cup plus 1 Tbsp coconut oil (warmed to liquid)
1/2 cup raw cacao powder
1 tsp chipotle powder
1 tsp cinnamon
1/2 teaspoon sea salt
1 Tbsp pure vanilla extract and seeds from half a vanilla bean (other half reserved for topping)

Caramel:
10 medjool dates, pitted
1 Tbsp almond butter
2 Tbsp agave nectar or honey
1/4 tsp sea salt
1 Tbsp coconut oil
1 tsp pure vanilla extract
2 Tbsp water

1 cup chopped Raw Pecan Pie Dark Chocolates (or other chopped raw chocolate)
1 cup chopped raw pecans

Lightly coat a 6 inch spring form removable bottom pan with coconut oil. To prepare the crust, process pecans, buckwheat and sea salt in a food processor until the pecans are fine crumbs, then add the dates and process until the mixture holds together when squeezed between your fingers (if not holding together, add more dates). Firmly press crust into the bottom of the prepared pan, and set aside.

To make the filling, drain the cashews and combine them with coconut water, agave nectar, raw cacao powder, chipotle powder, sea salt, and vanilla in a food processor, and blend until smooth and creamy. With the processor running, add the coconut oil, and process for a minute until blended. Set aside while you prepare caramel.

To make the caramel, combine all ingredients in the food processor and process until smooth, then press through a fine meshed strainer to remove any date bits (optional, but makes for a smoother caramel).

To assemble cheesecake, scatter about 2/3 of the chopped chocolates and pecans over the crust. Pour in half the chocolate filling and then drop some of the caramel by the teaspoonful over the filling. Pour the remaining chocolate filling over then drop more caramel on the top. Swirl the filling with a knife, and tap on the countertop to level. Place in the freezer to set for about 4-6 hours. Once set, decorate the edges of the top of the cake with the remaining chocolates and pecans. Serve! Store remaining cheesecake in the refrigerator.

Raw Lime Dark Chocolate Pistachio Cheesecake

Makes one 6 inch cake

Crust:

1/2 cup raw pistachios, soaked and dried

1/2 cup sprouted buckwheat, dried in the dehydrator (or additional coconut or pistachios)

1/2 cup dried finely shredded coconut

1/8 teaspoon sea salt

10-12 soft medjool dates, pitted and chopped

Filling:

1 cup raw cashews (preferably soaked overnight and drained)

1 cup diced avocado

1 cups young coconut meat (or additional soaked cashews if unavailable)

1/4 cup lime juice

2 Tbsp organic lime zest

1/4 cup coconut water (or filtered water)

1/2 cup raw coconut nectar, raw agave nectar or raw honey

1/2 cup plus 1 Tbsp raw coconut oil (warmed to liquid)

1/2 teaspoon sea salt

1 Tbsp pure vanilla extract and seeds from half a vanilla bean

1/4 cup raw cacao powder

1/4 cup chopped raw pistachios

For garnish, chopped raw chocolate, raw pistachios and a lime slice

Lightly coat a 6 inch spring form removable bottom pan with coconut oil. To prepare the crust, process pistachios, buckwheat, and sea salt in a food processor until the nuts are fine crumbs, then add the dates and process until the mixture holds together when squeezed between your fingers (if not holding together, add more dates). Firmly press crust into the bottom of the prepared pan, and set aside.

To make the filling, drain the cashews and combine them with avocadoes, coconut, lime juice, lime zest, coconut water, coconut nectar, sea salt, and vanilla in a food processor and blend until smooth and creamy. With the processor running, add the coconut oil, and process for a minute until blended. Remove half the filling from the food processor and place in a bowl. Add the cacao powder to the remaining half in the processor. Process until well blended and place in another bowl.

To assemble cheesecake, pour half the chocolate filling over the crust, and then scatter over 1/4 cup chopped pistachios. Pour the remaining chocolate filling over. Pour the lime filling over that and smooth the top. Place the cheesecake in the freezer to firm up for about 4 hours. Once ready to serve, scatter pistachios and raw chopped chocolate around the edge on top of the cake, and place a lime slice in the middle (or you can be creative and arrange it in your own way). Store leftover cake in the refrigerator.

Raw Samoa Cheesecake

Makes one 6 inch cake

Crust:
1/2 cup raw macadamia nuts, soaked and dried
1/2 cup sprouted buckwheat, dried in the dehydrator (or macadamia nuts)
1/2 cup dried finely shredded coconut
1/8 teaspoon sea salt
10-12 soft medjool dates, pitted and chopped
1 tsp pure vanilla extract

Filling:
1 1/2 cups raw cashews (preferably soaked overnight and drained)
1 1/2 cups young coconut meat (or additional soaked cashews if unavailable)
1/2 cup coconut water (or filtered water)
1/2 cup raw coconut nectar, raw agave nectar or raw honey
1/2 cup plus 1 Tbsp raw coconut oil (warmed to liquid)
1/2 teaspoon sea salt
1 Tbsp pure vanilla extract and seeds from half a vanilla bean (other half reserved for topping)

1/4 cup raw cacao powder
1/4 cup finely shredded coconut

Caramel:
15 medjool dates, pitted
3 Tbsp coconut butter
1/4 cup raw coconut nectar, raw agave nectar or raw honey
1/4 tsp sea salt
1 Tbsp coconut oil
2 tsp pure vanilla extract
1/4 cup water (or as needed)
1/4 cup finely shredded coconut

Raw Chocolate:
1/4 cup raw cacao powder
1/4 cup raw coconut oil
2 Tbsp raw coconut nectar or agave nectar
a pinch of sea salt

Lightly coat a 6 inch spring form removable bottom pan with coconut oil. To prepare the crust, process macadamias, buckwheat, and sea salt in a food processor until the nuts are fine crumbs, then add the dates and vanilla and process until the mixture holds together when squeezed between your fingers (if not holding together, add more dates). Firmly press crust into the bottom of the prepared pan, and set aside.

To make the filling, drain the cashews and combine them with coconut water, agave nectar, sea salt, and vanilla in a food processor and blend until smooth and creamy. With the processor running, add the coconut oil, and process for a minute until blended. Remove half the filling from the food processor and place in a bowl. Stir in 1/4 cup shredded coconut, and add the cacao powder to the remaining half in the processor. Process until well blended and place in another bowl. Set aside while you prepare caramel.

To make the caramel, combine all ingredients in the food processor, and process until smooth (adding more water by the tablespoonful if too thick), then press through a fine meshed strainer to remove any date bits (optional, but makes for a smoother caramel). Divide the caramel into 2 bowls, stirring 1/4 cup shredded coconut into one.

To assemble cheesecake, pour the vanilla coconut filling into the crust. Drop half the caramel without the coconut onto the top of it in teaspoonfuls, and swirl with a knife. Pour the chocolate filling over and drop the remaining caramel without the coconut over in the same fashion you did with the rest of it. Swirl with a knife. Place the cheesecake in the freezer to firm up for about 4 hours. Once it is firmed up, spread the caramel with the coconut over the top.

To make the chocolate, whisk together all ingredients in a bowl until well combined. Drizzle over the cheesecake (it is easier if you put it in a plastic bag and cut the tip off to drizzle it). Place the cake in the freezer for about 5 minutes to harden the chocolate. Serve.

Raw Ginger Carrot Dream Cakes

Makes four 4 inch cheesecakes

Crisp Sweet and Salty Carrots garnish (optional):
1 large carrot
agave nectar
fleur de sel

Crust:
1 1/2 cup shelled raw pistachios
1/8 teaspoon sea salt
8 soft medjool dates, pitted and chopped

Filling:
2 3/4 cups raw cashews (preferably soaked overnight)
1/2 cup coconut water (or filtered water)
1 Tbsp Lemon juice
1/3 cup plus 3 Tbsp agave nectar
2 inch piece fresh ginger, chopped
1/2 teaspoon sea salt
1 Tbsp pure vanilla extract and seeds from half a vanilla bean (other half reserved for topping)
1 cup chopped organic carrot
1/2 cup plus 1 Tbsp coconut oil (warmed to liquid)

caramel:
4 medjool dates
3 Tbsp almond butter
1/4 cup plus 2 Tbsp agave nectar
1 tsp maple extract
1/8 tsp fleur de sel
1 1/2 Tbsp filtered water if needed

pistachios for garnish

To make optional carrot chip garnish, slice carrots very thin on the diagonal, and coat with a little agave nectar. Place on trays in your food dehydrator, and dry for about 8 hours, or until crisp. Remove from the trays and sprinkle with a little fleur de sel. Set aside.

Lightly coat four 4 inch spring form removable bottom pans with coconut oil. To prepare the crust, process pistachios and sea salt in a food processor until the pecans are fine crumbs, and then add the dates and process until the mixture holds together when squeezed between your fingers. Firmly press crust into the bottoms of the prepared pans, and set aside.

To make the filling, drain the cashews and combine them with coconut water, lemon juice, agave nectar, ginger, sea salt, vanilla, and carrots in a food processor and blend until smooth and creamy. Slowly add the oil to the food processor with the motor running, and let process until well blended. Remove the filling from the food processor, and press through a fine mesh strainer (if a smoother result is desired). To assemble the cheesecake, pour the filling over the crusts, then place in the freezer until it is set, 4 to 6 hours, then once set store in the frigerator.

To make caramel, combine all ingredients in the food processor and process until smooth (add a little (1-2 Tbsp) water if necessary to make the caramel a pourable consistency). Drizzle a bit of the caramel over each cheesecake and top each with a few crisp carrot slices and some pistachios. Store leftover cake in the refrigerator.

Raw Banana Split Cake

Makes one 6 inch cake

Crust:
1/2 cup raw walnuts
1/2 cup sprouted buckwheat, dried in the dehydrator (or additional coconut)
1/2 cup dried finely shredded coconut
1/8 teaspoon sea salt
10-12 soft medjool dates, pitted and chopped

Filling:
2 cups raw cashews (preferably soaked overnight and drained)
2 cups young coconut meat (or 1 1/2 cups soaked cashews if coconut is unavailable)
1/2 cup coconut water
1/3 cup raw coconut nectar, raw agave nectar or raw honey
1/2 cup plus 2 Tbsp raw coconut oil (warmed to liquid)
1/2 teaspoon sea salt
1 Tbsp pure vanilla extract and seeds from half a vanilla bean
4 organic strawberries
3 Tbsp cacao powder
1 organic banana, sliced

Sauce/Swirls:
1/4 cup orgainc pineapple
2 medjool dates

1/2 cup organic strawberries
2 medjool dates

1/4 cup raw cacao
1/4 cup raw coconut nectar or agave nectar
2 tsp coconut oil
a pinch of sea salt

2 organic bananas, halved lengthwise, then the halves cut in half

1/4 cup diced pineapple
1/4 cup halved strawberries

Lightly coat a 6 inch spring form removable bottom pan with coconut oil. To prepare the crust, process walnuts, buckwheat, and sea salt in a food processor until the nuts are fine crumbs, then add the dates and process until the mixture holds together when squeezed between your fingers (if not holding together, add more dates). Firmly press crust into the bottom of the prepared pan, and set aside. To make the filling, drain the cashews and combine them with coconut, coconut water, coconut nectar, sea salt, and vanilla in a food processor, and blend until smooth and creamy. With the processor running, add the coconut oil, and process for a minute until blended. Divide into 3 bowls. Add one back to the food processor and add the strawberries. Blend until well combined, and then scrape back into the bowl. Add the second bowl to the food processor and add the 3 Tbsp cacao powder. Process until well blended, then scrape back into the bowl. Set the fillings aside in the refrigerator.

For the swirls and sauces, first, combine the pineapple in the food processor with 2 dates and process until smooth. Scrape into a small bowl and set aside. Next, combine the strawberries in a food processor with 2 dates, and process until smooth. Scrape into a bowl and set aside. In another small bowl, whisk together the cacao powder, coconut nectar, coconut oil and sea salt until the consistency of fudge sauce (if too thick, add a little more coconut oil; if too thin, add a little more cacao powder).

To assemble the cake, pour the chocolate filling over the prepared crust, then drop some of the chocolate sauce over it by the teaspoonful (reserving the rest for the topping) and swirl it with a knife. Next, top with a layer of sliced bananas. Then, pour the strawberry filling over, and drop some strawberry sauce over it by the teaspoonful (reserving the rest for the topping) and swirl it with a knife. Next, pour over the plain filling and drop some of the pineapple over it by the teaspoonful (reserving the rest of it for the topping) and swirl with a knife. Place the cake in the freezer to set for 4-6 hours until firm throughout.

Once the cake has set, unmold, put on a serving plate and top with the halved bananas, cut side down. Then, top with the diced pineapple, strawberries, and drizzle with some of each of the sauces. Serve.

Raw Spring Blossom Cake

Makes one 6 inch cake

Cake:
1/2 cup raw almond meal
2 cups raw coconut flour
1/4 tsp sea salt
1 tsp pure vanilla extract
12 medjool dates, pitted
2 cups coconut meat*
2 Tbsp coconut water
2 Tbsp fresh lime juice
2 Tbsp organic lime zest
2 Tbsp raw coconut nectar
 one large handful organic spinach

Cream topping:
2 1/3 cups raw cashew pieces (preferably soaked overnight)
2 1/3 cups fresh young coconut meat (or 1 3/4 cups soaked cashews if coconut meat is unavailable)
1/2 cup plus 2 Tbsp coconut water
1/2 cup raw coconut nectar, or your choice of raw liquid sweetener
1/2 tsp sea salt
1 Tbsp pure vanilla extract and seeds of a vanilla bean
1/2 cup plus 2 Tbsp raw coconut oil (warmed to liquid)
3 Tbsp coconut butter

2 Tbsp lemon juice
1 Tbsp lemon zest
turmeric, divided**
1/3 cup organic mango
1 small 1/2 tsp raw beet and 1 Tbsp raw beet**
1/3 cup organic strawberries
a small handful spinach

Topping:
about 10 sliced organic strawberries

1 Tbsp mango, diced small

Combine almond flour, coconut flour, and sea salt, in a bowl and whisk together until well blended. Set aside. To a food processor, add the dates, vanilla, coconut lime juice and zest, coconut water, nectar, and spinach to the processor and process until smooth. Add the dry ingredients back and process until smooth and well incorporated. Place the batter on a teflex lined dehydrator sheet, in slightly larger than a 6 inch circle and dehydrate for about 8 hours, until dried but still moist in the center. Once dried, trim into a 6 inch circle, place in the bottom of a 6 inch springform pan (greased with coconut oil), and set aside.

To make the cream topping, combine the cashews, coconut, coconut water, coconut nectar, sea salt, vanilla, and vanilla bean, and process until smooth. Add the coconut oil with the processor running to incorporate it completely. Once blended, divide the cream mixture into 4 bowls and set aside. To the first bowl, add the lemon zest, juice and a pinch of turmeric to the bowl and whisk to blend. Add the second bowl of cream back to the food processor and add the 1/3 cup mango, a small pinch of turmeric and a small piece of beet and process until blended then remove back to the bowl. Add the third bowl to the processor and add 1/3 cup strawberries and the 1 Tbsp raw beet and process until smooth and well blended. Add back to the bowl. Add the 4th bowl of cream back to the food processor and add the spinach. Process until smooth and add back to the bowl and place in the fridge.

To assemble the cake, drop the lemon filling, the mango filling and the strawberry filling by the tablespoonful randomly over the lime cake in the prepared pan. Once the pan is filled tap on the countertop to level and swirl with a knife (being sure to go to the bottom of the filling). Place in the freezer to set, about 3 hours. Once set, arrange the sliced strawberries on top of the cake to resemble a flower and place the diced mango in the middle. Place the green cream in a pastry bag (or a plastic bag with the end cut off), and decorate the sides of the cake, creating leaves and vines. Serve. Store extra cake in the refrigerator.

*If you cannot get fresh coconut meat, soak 2 cups dried coconut for 4 hours then drain. Continue with the cake recipe.
**The beets and turmeric are for coloring the cake more vividly, but if you do not have them you can substitute natural food coloring.

Raw Strawberry Short Cake

Makes one 6 inch cake

Cake:
1/2 cup raw almond meal
2 cups raw coconut flour
1/4 tsp sea salt
1 tsp pure vanilla extract
12 medjool dates, pitted
2 cups coconut meat*
1/4 cup coconut water
2 Tbsp raw coconut nectar

Cream topping:
2 cups raw cashew pieces (preferably soaked overnight)
2 cups fresh young coconut meat (or 1 3/4 cups soaked cashews if coconut meat is unavailable)
1/2 cup coconut water
1/4 cup plus 2 Tbsp raw coconut nectar, or your choice of raw liquid sweetener
1/2 tsp sea salt
1 Tbsp pure vanilla extract and seeds of a vanilla bean
1/2 cup raw coconut oil (warmed to liquid)
1/2 cup organic strawberries

8 organic strawberries halved (or enough to cover the cake layer)

Sauce:
1/2 cup organic strawberries
2 medjool dates

8 organic strawberries halved (or enough to cover the top of the cake.
Combine almond flour, coconut flour, and sea salt, in a bowl and whisk together until well blended. Set aside. To a food processor, add the dates, vanilla, coconut and coconut water, and nectar to the processor and process until smooth. Add the dry ingredients back and process until smooth and well incorporated. Place the batter on a teflex lined dehydrator sheet, in slightly larger than a 6 inch circle and dehydrate for about 8 hours, until dried but still moist in the center. Once dried,

trim into a 6 inch circle, place in the bottom of a 6 inch springform pan (greased with coconut oil), and set aside.

To make the cream topping, combine the cashews, coconut, coconut water, coconut nectar, sea salt, vanilla, vanilla bean, and process until smooth. Add the coconut oil with the processor running to incorporate it completely. Once blended, remove half the cream mixture and set aside in a bowl. Add the 1/2 cup strawberries to the remaining cream in the processor and process until smooth and well blended. Scoop into a bowl.

To assemble the cake, place 8 strawberries (or however many it takes to cover the cake layer) over the cake layer in the prepared pan cut side down. Pour the strawberry cream over it and smooth it out to the sides. Pour the vanilla cream over that, and smooth the top to the sides. Place in the freezer and allow to set until firm, about 3 hours or so.

While setting, make the strawberry sauce. Combine 1/2 cup strawberries with 2 medjool dates in the food processor and process until smooth.

Once the cake is set, top with the 8 halved strawberries (or however many it takes to cover the cake), and then spoon some of the sauce over. Serve.

*If you cannot get fresh coconut meat, soak 2 cups dried coconut for 4 hours then drain. Continue with the cake recipe.

Fragrant Vanilla Cake

The Ultimate Raw Carrot Cake
Makes one 6 inch cake

Carrot Cake:
1/2 cup raw sprouted oat flour or raw almond meal
1 cup raw coconut flour
1/4 tsp sea salt
1 tsp pure vanilla extract
12 medjool dates, pitted
1 inch chunk ginger
2 tsp cinnamon
1 tsp cardamom
3/4 cup dried shredded unsweetened coconut
1 1/2 cups grated organic carrots

Cheesecake filling:
1 1/2 cups raw cashew pieces (preferably soaked overnight)
2 cups fresh young coconut meat (or additional soaked cashews if not available)
1/3 cup raw coconut nectar, or raw agave nectar
1/2 tsp sea salt
1 Tbsp pure vanilla extract and seeds of half a vanilla bean
1/2 cup coconut water
1/2 cup plus 1 Tbsp raw coconut oil (warmed to liquid)

Carrot filling:
1/2 cup chopped organic carrots
1/2 inch piece ginger
1 tsp cinnamon
1/2 tsp cardamom

Cream Topping (optional):
1/2 cup young Thai coconut (or 1/2 cup soaked cashews if unavailable)
1/2 cup raw cashews (soaked for 4 hours and drained)
1/4 cup coconut water
2 Tbsp raw coconut nectar, or raw agave nectar
1/8 tsp sea salt

1 tsp pure vanilla extract
2 Tbsp raw coconut oil (warmed to liquid)

For the cake, in a food processor, combine the oat flour, coconut flour, sea salt, dates, vanilla, ginger, cinnamon, cardamom, and process until the dates are incorporated and it is all well blended. Add the coconut and 1 cup of the carrots and process until smooth. Add the remaining carrots and pulse until incorporated. Place the batter on a teflex lined dehydrator sheet, and dehydrate for about 8 hours, until dried but still moist in the center. Once dried, cut into a 6 inch circle, place in the bottom of a 6 inch springform pan (greased with coconut oil), and set aside.
To make the filling, combine the cashews, coconut meat, coconut nectar, sea salt, vanilla, and coconut water, and process until smooth. With the motor running, add the coconut oil slowly to incorporate it. Divide the filling into 2 bowls, and add one back to the dehydrator. Add the carrots, ginger, cinnamon, cardamom, and process until smooth (you may need to press through a fine meshed strainer to remove carrot bits for really smooth filling). Pour the carrot filling over the cake in the pan (reserving about 1/4 cup). Next pour over the plain filling. Drop the remaining carrot filling by the teaspoonful over the vanilla, tap the bottom on the countertop to level, then swirl with a knife or skewer. Place in the freezer to set, about 4-6 hours.
For the optional cream topping, combine all ingredients but the coconut oil in the food processor and process until smooth. With the motor running, add the coconut oil slowly and process for a minute until well incorporated. Remove from the processor and place in a bowl. Put the bowl in the freezer for about 45 minutes or until it is the consistency of frosting. Place in a pastry bag and pipe around the edges of the cake. Serve. Store extra cake in the refrigerator.

Raw Lemon Lavender Doughnuts
Makes 12

Doughnuts:
2 1/2 cups raw almond meal
2 1/2 cups dried shredded unsweetened coconut
1 cup sprouted buckwheat flour or additional coconut
2 Tbsp lemon zest
1/4 cup lemon juice
1/4 tsp sea salt
1 tsp pure vanilla extract
2/3 cup raw coconut nectar
2 drops du Terra lavender essential oil
1 Tbsp dried lavender flowers

Frosting:
3/4 cup raw cashew pieces (preferably soaked overnight)
2 Tbsp coconut water
2 Tbsp lemon juice
1 Tbsp lemon zest
1 cups fresh young coconut meat (or additional soaked cashews if not available)
3 Tbsp raw coconut nectar, raw agave nectar or raw honey
1/4 tsp sea salt
1 teaspoons vanilla and seeds of half a vanilla bean
2 drops du Terra lavender essential oil
1/4 cup raw coconut oil (warmed to liquid)
a few drops natural purple food coloring
dried lavender flowers for garnish

For the doughnuts, combine the almond meal, coconut, buckwheat flour, and sea salt in the food processor and process until finely ground like flour (but not too long or it will turn to nut butter). Add the lemon juice and zest, vanilla, coconut nectar, and lavender oil and process until smooth. Stir in lavender flowers until evenly blended. Form batter into 12 doughnuts on a lined dehydrator sheet. Dehydrate at 115 for about 8 hours, or until dry but still soft.
For the frosting, combine the cashews, coconut water, lemon juice and zest, coconut, coconut nectar, sea salt, vanilla, and lavender oil. Process until smooth.

With the motor running, add the coconut oil and process until blended. Add the food coloring and process until evenly colored. Place the frosting in a bowl and put it in the freezer for about 30 minutes to an hour (depending on how warm it has become) until it is chilled to frosting like consistency. Once chilled, place in a pastry bag (or plastic Ziploc with the corner cut off) and pipe onto doughnuts. Sprinkle with dried lavender and serve.

Raw Dark Chocolate Glazed Red Velvet Doughnuts

Makes 16

Doughnuts:
3 cups almond meal
2 1/2 cups dried shredded unsweetened coconut
1/2 tsp sea salt
1/4 cup plus 2 Tbsp agave nectar or honey
2 tsp pure vanilla extract
1 small 2 inch chunk of organic raw red beet (or enough to color the cake red)

Raw Chocolate Glaze:
1/2 cup melted coconut oil
1/2 cup raw cacao powder
a pinch sea salt
1/4 cup agave nectar

To make the doughnuts, combine all ingredients and process until smooth. Shape into 16 balls and then shape into doughnuts and place on a dehydrator sheet. Dry for about 8 hours or until not sticky. To make the glaze, whisk all ingredients until smooth. Let sit a little while to thicken. Place the doughnuts on a drying rack. Drizzle the glaze over the doughnuts, then set them on a foil lined sheet pan. Place in the freezer to harden for a few minutes. Remove from freezer, and serve.

Pies, Tarts and Pastry

Who doesn't like pie? Apple pie is classic, but I tend to make the more unusual ones such as Raw Banana Macadamia Coconut Dream Pie or Chocolate Strawberry Silk. When I am in a lighter mood however, nothing beats a tart filled with lemon curd, or a crumble topping over fruit. In this chapter you will find pies and tarts for all seasons of the year, and even a recipe for baklava.

Raw Chocolate Strawberry Silk Pie
Makes one 6 inch pie

Crust:
1 cup finely shredded dried coconut
3/4 cup sprouted dehydrated buckwheat groats (or additional coconut)
1 cup raw pecans
10 soft medjool dates, pitted (if not soft, soak them 30 minutes and drain well)
1/4 tsp sea salt
1/4 cup raw cacao powder

chocolate mousse Filling:
2 cups diced ripe avocados (about 3 medium)
1/4 cup plus 1 Tbsp raw coconut nectar, or your choice of raw liquid sweetener
1/4 tsp sea salt
1/2 Tbsp pure vanilla extract
1/4 cup plus 2 Tbsp raw cacao powder
3 Tbsp coconut butter, liquified

about 3 sliced organic strawberries

 strawberry cream topping:
1 cup raw cashew pieces (preferably soaked overnight)
1 cup fresh young coconut meat packed (or 1 cup soaked cashews if coconut meat is unavailable)
1/4 cup fresh coconut water
3 Tbsp raw coconut nectar, or your choice of raw liquid sweetener
1/4 tsp sea salt
1/2 Tbsp pure vanilla extract and seeds of a vanilla bean
1/4 cup   plus 1 Tbsp raw coconut oil (warmed to liquid)
1 cup fresh strawberries

1/4 cup chopped raw chocolate
2 strawberries, cut into 8ths (wedges)

For the crust, combine all ingredients in the food processor until finely chopped and starting to hold together when squeezed (if it doesn't you may need a few more dates). Press the mixture into a 6 inch pie pan or spring form pan greased with coconut oil. Place in the refrigerator while you make the fillings.

For the mousse, combine all ingredients in the food processor and process until smooth. Pour into the pie crust and top with the sliced berries. Place in the refrigerator to set.

To make the strawberry cream, combine the cashews, coconut, coconut water, coconut nectar, sea salt, and vanilla. Process until smooth. Add the coconut oil with the motor running and process for a minute. Add the berries and process until smooth. Place in a bowl, and put in the freezer for about 45 minutes until it is the consistency of whipped cream.

Top with the chopped chocolate and sliced berries and place in the refrigerator for about an hour to chill before serving. Store in the refrigerator.

Raw Banana Macadamia Coconut Dream Pie

Makes one 6 inch tart

Crust:
1 cup macadamia nuts
1 cups shredded, dried coconut
1/2 cup sprouted, dried buckwheat (or additional coconut
1/8 teaspoon sea salt
8 soft medjool dates, pitted and chopped

Filling:
2 cups sliced bananas
1/2 cup raw cashews (soaked for at least 4 hours in filtered water and drained)
1/3 cup coconut water
1 1/2 cups young coconut meat or soaked cashews (drained)
1/3 cup plus 1 Tbsp raw agave nectar or raw honey
1/4 tsp sea salt
2 tsp pure vanilla extract and seeds from half a vanilla bean (other half reserved for topping)
1/3 cup raw coconut oil (warmed to liquid)
2 sliced bananas
3 Tbsp raw cacao powder

Cream topping:
3/4 cup raw cashew pieces (preferably soaked overnight)
1/4 cup coconut water
1 cups fresh young coconut meat (or additional soaked cashews if not available)
3 Tbsp raw agave nectar or raw honey
1/4 tsp sea salt
1 teaspoons vanilla and seeds of half a vanilla bean
1/4 cup raw coconut oil (warmed to liquid)
1/2 cup raw macadamia nuts
1/2 cup large flake coconut
large pinch of sea salt
1 Tbsp honey

For the crust, combine the nuts, coconut, and buckwheat in a food processor and process until crumbs. Add the sea salt and dates and process until the mixture starts to come together when squeezed. Press into the bottom and up the sides of a 6 inch springform pan, sprayed with non-stick coconut oil spray. Place in the freezer while you prepare the filling.

For the filling, combine 2 cups bananas, coconut, cashews, coconut water, agave, sea salt, and vanilla in a food processor and process until smooth. With the motor running, slowly add the coconut oil and process for a minute. Divide the mixture into 2 bowls, then place one back in the food processor and add cacao powder. Process until combined. Pour the chocolate filling mixture over the prepared crust, then top with sliced bananas, then the plain filling, then more bananas. Place in the freezer to set for about an hour.

Meanwhile, to make the topping, combine the cashews, coconut, coconut water, sea salt, agave nectar, and vanilla. Process until smooth. Add the coconut oil slowly with the motor running (If the mixture starts to separate and clump, the filling is too cold to emulsify the oil, so warm some of it and process again). Place the topping in the freezer for about 30-45 minutes until it firms up to whipped cream consistency. Once frosting consistency, move to the refrigerator until ready to use.
Once the filling has set, spread over the tart.
In a food processor, place macadamia nuts, coconut, sea salt, and honey, and pulse until chopped. Sprinkle over tart, and serve. Store extra in the refrigerator.

Mini Raw Sweet Potato Caramel Pecan Pies

Makes two 4 inch pies

Crust:
1 1/2 cups pecans
1 1/2 cups sprouted, dehydrated buckwheat (or additional pecans)
1/8 teaspoon sea salt
12 soft medjool dates, pitted and chopped

Filling:
2 cups raw sweet potatoes or yams, cubed
1/2 cup young coconut meat or soaked cashews (drained)
2 Tbsp coconut butter
1/4 cup coconut water (or filtered water)
1/3 cup plus 1 Tbsp agave nectar or honey
1/4 tsp sea salt
2 tsp pure vanilla extract and seeds from half a vanilla bean (other half reserved for topping)
1 inch piece fresh ginger
1 tsp cardamom
2 tsp cinnamon
1/2 tsp nutmeg
1/4 cup raw coconut oil (warmed to liquid)

Caramel:
10 medjool dates, pitted
1 Tbsp almond butter
2 Tbsp agave nectar or honey
1/4 tsp sea salt
1 Tbsp coconut oil
1 tsp pure vanilla extract
2 Tbsp water

1 cup raw pecan halves

Spray two 4 inch pie or tart pans lined with plastic wrap to make removal easier.
To prepare the crust, process pecans, buckwheat, and sea salt in a food processor,

until the pecans are fine crumbs, then add the dates and process until the mixture holds together when squeezed between your fingers. Firmly press crust into the bottoms of the pans, and set aside in the freezer to firm up.

To make the filling, combine the sweet potatoes, coconut meat, coconut water, nectar, spices, sea salt, and vanilla. Blend until smooth and creamy. Add the coconut oil with the processor running to evenly distribute it, and process for about a minute. If desired, press the filling mixture through a fine mesh strainer to remove any sweet potato bits (you can skip this but the filling may not be as smooth.) Pour the filling into the two prepared crusts. Place in the freezer until it is set, about 2 hours.

To make the caramel, combine all ingredients in the food processor and process until smooth, then press through a fine mesh strainer to remove any date bits (optional, but makes for a smoother caramel).

Once pies have set, arrange the pecans decoratively on top of the pies. Place caramel in a pastry bag and pipe over the top in a crisscross fashion. Serve.

Blueberry Rhubarb Ginger Crumble Tart

Makes one 8 inch tart

Crust:
2 cups raw pecans
2 cups finely shredded dried coconut
1 1/2 cup buckwheat groats, sprouted and dehydrated (or additional coconut)
1/2 tsp sea salt
1/4 cup plus 2 Tbsp raw cacao powder
24 soft medjool dates, pitted (if not soft, soak them until they are and drain them)

Topping:
3/4 cup chopped raw pecans
1/2 cup flaked coconut

Filling:
2 cups rhubarb, cut into 1/2 inch pieces
2 Tbsp raw coconut nectar or raw agave nectar

2 cups organic blueberries
2 Tbsp. chia seeds
a pinch sea salt
1 inch piece fresh ginger
2 Tbsp raw coconut nectar or raw agave nectar
1 tsp pure vanilla extract

For the crust, combine all ingredients in a food processor and process until fine crumbs and starting to hold together when squeezed. Press 2/3 of the mixture into the bottom of an 8 inch removable bottom tart pan, and set aside in the refrigerator. Combine the remaining crust mixture with 3/4 cup chopped pecans, 1/2 cup flaked coconut and toss well. Set aside in the refrigerator. This will be the topping.
Toss the rhubarb with 2 Tbsp raw coconut nectar and spread out on a foil lined dehydrator tray. Tent another piece of foil over the top, and dehydrate at 115 degrees for 4-5 hours, until it is tender. Once it has "cooked" combine it with the

blueberries in a bowl, and toss to combine. Remove 2/3 cup of the mixture and place in the dehydrator with the chia seeds, sea salt, ginger, 2 Tbsp coconut nectar, and vanilla. Process until smooth. Dump back into the bowl with the berries and rhubarb, and toss well. Pour the mixture into the tart crust and spread to the sides, then scatter the reserved topping over it. Let the pie sit in the refrigerator for 1 hour to allow flavor to develop and filling to set and then serve.

Raw Lime Avocado Tart

Makes one 6 inch tart

Crust:
1 cup macadamia nuts
1 cups shredded, dried coconut
1/2 cup sprouted, dried buckwheat (or additional coconut
1/8 teaspoon sea salt
8 soft medjool dates, pitted and chopped

Filling:
1 1/2 cups avocado
1 1/2 cups young coconut meat or soaked cashews (drained)
1/4 cup lime juice
2 Tbsp organic lime zest
1/3 cup plus 1 Tbsp agave nectar or honey
1/4 tsp sea salt
2 tsp pure vanilla extract and seeds from half a vanilla bean (other half reserved for topping)
1/4 cup raw coconut oil (warmed to liquid)

Cream topping:
3/4 cup raw cashew pieces (preferably soaked overnight)
1/4 cup coconut water
1 cups fresh young coconut meat (or additional soaked cashews if not available)
3 Tbsp raw agave nectar or raw honey
1/4 tsp sea salt
1 teaspoons vanilla and seeds of half a vanilla bean
1/4 cup raw coconut oil (warmed to liquid)

For the crust, combine the nuts, coconut, and buckwheat in a food processor and process until crumbs. Add the sea salt and dates and process until the mixture starts to come together when squeezed. Press into the bottom and up the sides of a 6 inch springform pan sprayed with non-stick coconut oil spray. Place in the freezer while you prepare the filling.
For the filling, combine avocado, coconut, lime juice and zest, honey, sea salt, and vanilla in a food processor. Process until smooth. With the motor running, slowly

add the coconut oil and process for a minute. Pour the filling into the crust, and place in the freezer for about 2 hours to firm up.

Meanwhile, to make the topping, combine the cashews, coconut water, sea salt, honey, and vanilla. Process until smooth. Add the coconut oil slowly with the motor running (If the mixture starts to separate and clump, the filling is too cold to emulsify the oil, so warm some of it and process again). Place the topping in the freezer for about 30-45 minutes until it firms up to frosting consistency. Once frosting consistency, move to the refrigerator until ready to use.

Once the filling has set, place the topping in a pastry bag and pipe decoratively over the tart. Serve. Store extra in the refrigerator.

Raw Little Lemon Tart with Lemon Almond Poppyseed Ice Cream

Makes two 4 inch tarts

2 4 inch removable bottom tart pans
crusts:
2/3 cup finely shredded dried coconut
1/3 cup sprouted, dehydrated buckwheat (or additional coconut)
1 cup almond meal or pulp (dehydrated)
6-8 medjool dates, pitted
1/4 tsp sea salt

lemon curd:
1/4 cup plus 2 Tbsp very hot filtered water
1 Tbsp flaked agar agar
1/2 cup lemon juice
zest of one organic lemon
2 Tbsp raw coconut nectar , raw agave nectar or raw local honey
1 tsp pure vanilla extract
3 Tbsp raw coconut butter
1 Tbsp raw coconut oil

lemon slices
Raw Lemon Almond Poppyseed Ice Cream (recipe follows)

To make the crust, combine all the ingredients in a food processor and process until finely chopped and starting to hold together. Press the mixture into two 4 inch removable bottom tart pans sprayed with non-stick spray. Place in the freezer while you prepare the curd.

For the curd, place the agar in the hot water in a bowl, and stir to dissolve. Once dissolved, let cool to room temperature and add other ingredients. Pour into a blender and blend until smooth. Pour into the prepared crusts and place in the fridge for about 4-6 hours or until set and chilled. Once chilled, garnish with a lemon slice, and serve with raw lemon almond poppyseed ice cream.

Raw Lemon Almond Poppyseed Ice Cream
Makes about 4 cups

1/2 cup lemon juice
1/2 cup almond milk
2 Tbsp organic lemon zest
2 cups raw cashews, soaked overnight and drained
2 cups young coconut meat, chopped
1/2 cup raw coconut nectar or raw agave nectar or raw honey
seeds of one vanilla bean
1 tsp pure almond extract
a pinch of sea salt
1/2 cup coconut oil, warmed to liquid
2 Tbsp black poppyseeds

Add lemon juice and almond milk to a food processor, along with zest, cashews, coconut meat, coconut nectar, vanilla, almond extract, and sea salt. Process until smooth. Then with the processor running, add the coconut oil slowly and process until well incorporated, about a minute. Pour the mixture through a fine mesh strainer and press through, until you have removed any coconut bits (you can skip this step, but it makes for a smoother ice cream). Stir in poppy seeds, and pour the strained mixture into an ice cream maker, and process according to directions. Remove from ice cream maker, and pour into a freezer safe container. Let chill in the freezer for a few hours until a little more firm before scooping.

Raw Little Key Lime Tart with Strawberry Lime Ice Cream

Makes two 4 inch tarts

2 4 inch removable bottom tart pans
crusts:
2/3 cup finely shredded dried coconut
1/3 cup sprouted, dehydrated buckwheat (or additional coconut)
1 cup almond meal or pulp (dehydrated)
6-8 medjool dates, pitted
1/4 tsp sea salt

lime curd:
1/4 cup plus 2 Tbsp very hot filtered water
1 Tbsp flaked agar agar
1/2 cup lime juice
zest of two organic limes
2 Tbsp raw coconut nectar , raw agave nectar or raw local honey
1 tsp pure vanilla extract
3 Tbsp raw coconut butter
1 Tbsp raw coconut oil
a few spinach leaves (to tint green)

lime slices
Raw Strawberry Lime Ice Cream (recipe follows)

To make the crust, combine all the ingredients in a food processor and process until finely chopped and starting to hold together. Press the mixture into 2 four inch removable bottom tart pans sprayed with non-stick spray. Place in the freezer while you prepare the curd.

For the curd, place the agar in the hot water in a bowl, and stir to dissolve. Once dissolved, let cool to room temperature and add other ingredients. Pour into a blender and blend until smooth. Pour into the prepared crusts and place in the fridge for about 4-6 hours or until set and chilled. Once chilled, garnish with a lime slice, and serve with raw strawberry lime ice cream.

Raw Strawberry Lime Ice Cream
Makes about 5 cups

1/2 cup lime juice
1/2 cup fresh coconut water (or filtered water)
2 Tbsp organic lime zest
2 cups raw cashews, soaked overnight and drained
2 cups young coconut meat, chopped
1/2 cup raw coconut nectar or raw agave nectar or raw honey
seeds of one vanilla bean
a pinch of sea salt
1/2 cup coconut oil, warmed to liquid
2 cups organic strawberries

Add lime juice and coconut water to a food processor, along with zest, cashews, coconut meat, coconut nectar, vanilla, and sea salt. Process until smooth, then with the processor running, add the coconut oil slowly and process until well incorporated, about a minute. Add the berries and process until smooth. Pour the mixture through a fine mesh strainer and press through until you have removed any coconut bits (you can skip this step, but it makes for a smoother ice cream). Pour the strained mixture into an ice cream maker and process according to directions. Remove from ice cream maker, and pour into a freezer safe container. Let chill in the freezer for a few hours until a little more firm before scooping.

Raw Baklava with Saffron Ice Cream
Serves 2

"Filo" sheets:
1 large organic apple
1/2 cup almond meal
a pinch of sea salt
1 tsp raw agave nectar or honey
1/4 tsp ground cinnamon

Filling:
1 cup walnuts
6 dates
1 cup large flake coconut
1/4 tsp cinnamon
1/4 tsp rosewater
2 Tbsp raw agave nectar or honey plus additional for serving

For the "filo sheets", combine the apple, almond meal, sea salt, agave nectar, and cinnamon in a food processor and process until smooth. Spread out thinly onto a teflex lined dehydrator sheet in a large square. Dry for a few hours, or until not tacky anymore, then score into 9 squares. Place back in the dehydrator for about another 6-8 hours or until very crispy. Remove squares (you will have one extra to snack on).
For the filling, combine walnuts, dates, coconut, cinnamon, and rosewater in a food processor, and pulse until well combined but not pureed. You should still have chunks. Add 2 Tbsp agave nectar and pulse a few more times. Remove from the food processor.
To assemble, set out 2 plates. Drizzle each with a bit of the agave nectar or honey. Place one filo square on each, and top with 1/3 of the walnut mixture (dividing evenly between the two). Top each with another square, then half the remaining filling (dividing evenly between the two). Then add another square, then the rest of the filling then another square. Drizzle each baklava with a bit more agave nectar or honey, and scoop some saffron ice cream beside each (recipe follows). Enjoy.

Raw Saffron Ice Cream:
a large pinch saffron
1/2 cup coconut water
1 cup raw cashews, soaked overnight and drained
1 cup young coconut meat, chopped
1/4 cup raw agave nectar or raw honey
1 tsp rosewater
seeds of one vanilla bean
a pinch of sea salt
1/4 cup coconut oil, warmed to liquid

Warm the coconut water to 100 degrees or so, and place the saffron in it to steep. Let sit until cooled. Add to a food processor, along with cashews, coconut meat, agave nectar, rosewater, vanilla, and sea salt. Process until smooth, then with the processor running, add the coconut oil slowly and process until well incorporated, about a minute. Pour the mixture into an ice cream maker and process according to directions. Remove from ice cream maker, and pour into a freezer safe container. Let chill in the freezer for a few hours until a little more firm before scooping.

Ice Cream

I like to eat ice cream any time of the year, even when it is winter and I am staring out at the snow. It is something I make almost every week, and I enjoy coming up with new flavors. Once you make your own raw ice cream at home, you will never want to go back to store bought!

Raw Red Velvet Chocolate Chunk Ice Cream

Makes about 5 cups

Ice Cream:
1 cup coconut water
2 cups young coconut meat (or raw cashews, soaked 4 hours and drained if unavailable)
2 cups soaked raw cashews, drained (soaked at least 4 hours)
1/2 cup raw agave nectar or raw honey or raw coconut nectar
seeds of one vanilla bean
a pinch of sea salt
1/2 cup coconut oil, warmed to liquid
3 inch chunk organic raw beet

1 cup chopped raw chocolate

Add coconut water to a food processor, along with cashews, coconut, agave nectar, vanilla, and sea salt. Process until smooth, then with the processor running, add the coconut oil slowly and process until well incorporated, about a minute. Remove 1/3 of the mixture and place in a bowl in the fridge. Add the beet to the remaining mixture in the food processor and process until well blended. Pour through a fine mesh strainer to remove any coconut or beet bits. Pour the strained mixture into an ice cream maker and process according to directions. Remove from ice cream maker, stir in chocolate, and pour 1/3 of it into a freezer safe container with a lid, then add some of the plain vanilla mixture in tablespoonfuls. Add half the remaining red ice cream, then more drops of vanilla. Add the rest of the red mixture, then the last of the vanilla. Swirl with a knife. Set in the freezer for about 4 hours, or overnight before serving.

Raw Strawberry Rhubarb Ginger Ice Cream
Makes about 6 cups

Ice Cream:
1 cup coconut water
2 cups organic strawberries
1 cup organic rhubarb cut into 1 inch pieces
1 1/2 inch piece fresh ginger
2 cups young coconut meat (or raw cashews, soaked 4 hours and drained if unavailable)
2 cups soaked raw cashews, drained (soaked at least 4 hours)
1/2 cup raw coconut nectar or raw honey or raw agave nectar
seeds of one vanilla bean
a pinch of sea salt
1/2 cup coconut oil, warmed to liquid

Add coconut water to a food processor, along with strawberries, rhubarb, ginger, cashews, coconut, nectar, vanilla, and sea salt. Process until smooth, then with the processor running, add the coconut oil slowly and process until well incorporated, about a minute. Pour the strained mixture into an ice cream maker and process according to directions. Remove from ice cream maker, and pour into a freezer safe container with a lid. Let sit in the freezer for at least four hours or overnight to firm up to scoopable consistency.

Raw Sunshine Ice Cream
(carrot mango ginger ice cream)
Makes about 6 cups

Ice Cream:
1 cup orange juice
2 Tbsp organic orange zest
2 cups organic mango, diced
3/4 cup raw grated carrots
1 inch piece fresh ginger
2 cups young coconut meat (or raw cashews, soaked 4 hours and drained if unavailable)
2 cups soaked raw cashews, drained (soaked at least 4 hours)
1/2 cup raw agave nectar or raw honey or raw coconut nectar
seeds of one vanilla bean
a pinch of sea salt
1/2 cup coconut oil, warmed to liquid

Add orange juice and zest to a food processor, along with mango, carrots, ginger, cashews, coconut, agave nectar, vanilla, and sea salt. Process until smooth, then with the processor running, add the coconut oil slowly and process until well incorporated, about a minute. Pour the strained mixture into an ice cream maker and process according to directions. Remove from ice cream maker, and pour into a freezer safe container with a lid. Let sit in the freezer for at least four hours or overnight to firm up to scoopable consistency.

Raw Blueberry Lavender Ice Cream
Makes about 6 cups

Ice Cream:
1 cup coconut water
2 cups organic blueberries
2 cups young coconut meat (or raw cashews, soaked 4 hours and drained if unavailable)
2 cups soaked raw cashews, drained (soaked at least 4 hours)
1/2 cup raw agave nectar or raw honey or raw coconut nectar
seeds of one vanilla bean
2 drops du Terra lavender oil
a pinch of sea salt
1/2 cup coconut oil, warmed to liquid
2 Tbsp dried lavender flowers

Add coconut water, to a food processor, along with berries, cashews, coconut, agave nectar, vanilla, lavender oil, and sea salt. Process until smooth, then with the processor running, add the coconut oil slowly and process until well incorporated, about a minute. Stir lavender into the base. Pour into an ice cream maker and process according to directions. Remove from ice cream maker, and pour into a freezer safe container with a lid. Let sit in the freezer for at least four hours or overnight to firm up to scoopable consistency.

Raw Key Lime Pie Ice Cream

Makes about 6 cups

Pie crust chunks:
1/3 cup shredded coconut
1/3 cup raw pecans
1/4 cup sprouted raw buckwheat groats , dehydrated
1/8 tsp sea salt
4 medjool dates, pitted

Ice Cream:
1/2 cup coconut water
1/2 cup lime juice
1 Tbsp organic lime zest
1 cup young coconut meat (or raw cashews, soaked 4 hours and drained if unavailable)
1 cup diced avocado
2 cups soaked raw cashews, drained (soaked at least 4 hours)
1/2 cup raw agave nectar or raw honey or raw coconut nectar
seeds of one vanilla bean
a pinch of sea salt
1/2 cup coconut oil, warmed to liquid

To make pie crust chunks, combine all ingredients in a food processor and process until finely ground and holds together when squeezed. Form into small chunks and place in a bowl. Place in the freezer until hard.

Add coconut water and lime juice and zest to a food processor, along with cashews, avocado, coconut, agave nectar, vanilla, and sea salt. Process until smooth, then with the processor running, add the coconut oil slowly and process until well incorporated, about a minute. Pour the strained mixture into an ice cream maker and process according to directions. Remove from ice cream maker, and pour into a freezer safe container with a lid. Let sit in the freezer for at least four hours or overnight to firm up to scoopable consistency.

Candy

When it comes to candy, chocolate has always been my favorite. Chocolate filled with things like peanut butter and caramel that is. So I have included a lot of chocolate in this chapter, but since all raw candy is delicious to me, you will also find some of my favorite macaroons and fudges as well.

Raw Peanut Butter Caramel Cups

Makes 28 mini cups

Chocolate:
1 cup raw coconut oil, warmed to liquid
1 cup raw cacao powder
1/2 cup raw coconut nectar or agave nectar
a pinch sea salt

Peanut Butter:
3/4 cup raw peanut butter (or unsweetened pb if you are not concerned with being raw)
2 Tbsp raw coconut nectar

Caramel:
10 medjool dates
2 Tbsp raw coconut butter or macadamia butter (raw almond butter will also work)
3 Tbsp raw coconut nectar or agave nectar
1 tsp maple extract
1 Tbsp pure vanilla extract
1 Tbsp coconut oil
1/4 tsp fleur de sel
1/4 cup filtered water (or more if too thick, add an additional Tbsp at a time)

To make the chocolate, whisk all ingredients together until smooth, and set aside. In a small bowl, mix together the peanut butter and 2 tsp coconut nectar and set aside.
To make the caramel, combine all ingredients together in the food processor and process until smooth. You may need to add a little more water if too thick. Set aside.
Lay out 28 mini PB cup tins or molds on a flat cutting board or tray, and fill them about 1/3 full with the chocolate. Place them in the freezer to set about 5 minutes. Once set, spoon about 1 tsp of peanut butter onto each, followed by 1/2 tsp of caramel, smoothing it down slightly, but not so much that it oozes to the sides (you want to be able to cover it with more chocolate and not have it stick out the top). Spoon chocolate over each mound of caramel and PB enough to cover, and fill to the top of the tins. Place in the freezer to set for about 15-20 min. Enjoy.

Chipotle Caramel Dark Chocolates
Makes about 16

Caramel:
10 medjool dates
2 Tbsp raw coconut butter or macadamia butter (raw almond butter will also work)
3 Tbsp raw agave nectar or honey
1 tsp maple extract
1 Tbsp pure vanilla extract1 Tbsp coconut oil
1/4 tsp fleur de sel
2 tsp ground chipotle powder (or to taste)
1/4 cup filtered water (or more if too thick, add an additional Tbsp at a time)

Chocolate:
1/2 cup raw cacao powder
1/2 cup coconut oil, warmed to liquid
1/4 cup raw agave nectar
1/4 tsp ground chipotle powder
a pinch of sea salt

16 hole chocolate mold (I used silicone)

To make the caramel, combine all ingredients in a food processor and process until smooth (less chipotle powder if you want them more mild). Press the mixture thorough a fine mesh strainer to remove any date bits. Place into a pastry bag and pipe small 1/2 tsp mounds onto a piece of foil. Place in the freezer until hardened slightly.
When caramel is frozen, to make the chocolate, combine all ingredients and whisk together until smooth. Take your chocolate mold and fill holes half full with chocolate. Take your caramel and spoon one mound into each hole on top of the chocolate. Top with remaining chocolate in the holes so it is even with the top of the mold. Place in the freezer to harden, then pop out of the molds and enjoy.

Lavender Lemon Caramel Dark Chocolates
Makes about 16

Caramel:
10 medjool dates
2 Tbsp raw coconut butter or macadamia butter (raw almond butter will also work)
3 Tbsp raw agave nectar or honey
1 Tbsp pure vanilla extract

1 Tbsp coconut oil
1/4 tsp fleur de sel
1/4 cup lemon juice
1 Tbsp lemon zest
filtered water as needed
1 1/2 Tbsp dried lavender flowers

Chocolate:
1/2 cup raw cacao powder
1/2 cup coconut oil, warmed to liquid
1/4 cup raw agave nectar
a pinch of sea salt

16 hole chocolate mold (I used silicone)

To make the caramel, combine all ingredients (except lavender) in a food processor and process until smooth. Add a Tbsp or more of water if too thick. Press the mixture thorough a fine meshed strainer to remove any date bits. Stir in lavender. Place into a pastry bag and pipe small 1/2 tsp mounds onto a piece of foil. Place in the freezer until hardened slightly.
When caramel is frozen, to make the chocolate, combine all ingredients and whisk together until smooth. Take your chocolate mold and fill holes half full with chocolate. Take your caramel and spoon one mound into each hole on top of the chocolate. Top with remaining chocolate in the holes so it is even with the top of the mold. Place in the freezer to harden, then pop out of the molds and enjoy.

Raw Raspberry Rose Cream Truffles

Makes about 2 dozen

Raspberry Filling:
1 1/2 cups raw cashew pieces (soaked)
1/4 cup filtered water
1/4 cup raw coconut or agave nectar or raw honey
1/4 tsp sea salt
2 teaspoons vanilla and seeds of half a vanilla bean
1 tsp rosewater
1/4 cup raw coconut oil (warmed to liquid)
1 1/2 cups organic raspberries (if using frozen, thaw and drain liquid very well)

Chocolate:
1/2 cup raw cacao powder
1/2 cup raw coconut oil
1/4 cup raw coconut nectar or agave nectar
a pinch of sea salt

For the filling, in a food processor, combine the cashews, water, coconut nectar, sea salt, vanilla, and rosewater and process until smooth. With the processor running, add the coconut oil and process another minute until well incorporated. Add the raspberries and process until smooth. Pour into a bowl, and place in the freezer until firm, but scoopable. Scoop some of the cream out of the bowl by the heaping tablespoonful, and form into balls. Place on foil, and once they are all rolled, place back in the freezer to harden.

Meanwhile, make the chocolate. In a bowl, whisk together the cacao powder, coconut oil, coconut nectar, and sea salt until smooth. Allow to set until the mixture cools and thickens slightly.
Dip the filling balls into the chocolate and place on the foil. Once they are all dipped, place them back in the freezer to set completely. Enjoy. Store extra in the freezer.

Raw Key Lime Pie Truffles
makes about 16

1/2 cup cashews, soaked 4 hours
1/4 cup plus 2 Tbsp coconut butter
1/2 cup fresh lime juice
1 Tbsp lime zest
4 Tbsp raw agave nectar, to taste
pinch of salt
a handful of spinach

Chocolate coating:
1/2 cup raw cacao powder
1/2 cup raw coconut oil
1/4 cup raw coconut nectar or agave nectar
a pinch of sea salt

Drain and rinse cashews. Place in a food processor or high speed blender. Add coconut butter, lime juice, and zest, agave nectar and sea salt. Blend until smooth. Add spinach and blend until well combined. Place in a bowl in the fridge and chill for a few hours until firm enough to scoop. Scoop out balls by the heaping teaspoonful and place on a foil lined sheet and place in the freezer until firm (about an hour), then reshape to make smoother balls. Leave the balls in the freezer while you make the coating.

To make the coating, whisk together all ingredients until smooth in a bowl. Let sit until slightly more firm then dip the truffles into it, using a fork so the excess chocolate can drain off and place them back on the foil. Once they are all dipped, place in the freezer for about 5 minutes until the coating has hardened. Store truffles in the fridge.

Raw Coconut Rose Pistachio Macaroons
Makes 12

Macaroons:
3/4 cup raw almond meal*
a pinch of sea salt
1/4 cup raw agave nectar (or raw coconut nectar or raw honey)
1 small 1/2 inch chunk beet
1 tsp rosewater
1 tsp pure vanilla extract
2 cups finely shredded unsweetened coconut

Glaze:
1/4 cup coconut butter warmed to liquid
3 Tbsp coconut oil, warmed to liquid
1 Tbsp coconut nectar

1/2 cup chopped raw pistachios

Place almond meal, sea salt, agave nectar, beet, rosewater, and vanilla in the food
processor and process until well combined. Add coconut and pulse until the
mixture holds together. Form the mixture into 12 balls, and place on a dehydrator
sheet. Dehydrate for about 12 hours, or until they are dried, but not so much so that
they are not a little chewy in the middle.
To make the glaze, whisk together all ingredients until smooth. Dip a macaroon
into the glaze, then dip it into the pistachios. Place on a foil lined baking sheet or
plate. Repeat with remaining macaroons and once they are all dipped, place them
in the freezer to set for about 5 minutes before serving.

Raw Lavender Lemon Macaroons

Makes a dozen

Macaroons:
3/4 cup raw almond meal*
1 Tbsp lemon zest
2 Tbsp lemon juice
a pinch of sea salt
1/4 cup raw agave nectar
2 cups finely shredded unsweetened coconut
1 1/2 Tbsp dried lavender

Chocolate:
1/4 cup raw cacao powder
1/4 cup raw coconut oil
2 Tbsp raw agave nectar
a pinch of sea salt

Place almond meal, lemon zest, lemon juice, and sea salt in the food processor and process until well combined. Add the agave nectar and process until the mixture holds together. Add coconut and pulse until the mixture holds together, then add lavender and pulse until well distributed. Form the mixture into 12 balls, and place on a dehydrator sheet. Dehydrate for about 12 hours, or until they are dried, but not so much that they are not a little chewy in the middle.

To make chocolate, whisk all ingredients together until smooth in a bowl, and let sit until it thickens a little (about 15-20 min). Lay out a sheet of foil on a sheet pan. Dip each macaroon into the chocolate and place on the foil. Once all are dipped, put in the freezer to set. Once chocolate has hardened, enjoy.

Raw Strawberries and Cream Fudge
makes about 12 hearts (or 16 squares)

3 cups dried, finely shredded coconut
 1/2 cup coconut nectar
1/2 tsp sea salt
1 Tbsp pure vanilla extract
4 Tbsp raw macadamia butter or raw almond butter
1 cup fresh organic strawberries

 In a blender, grind one cup of the shredded coconut to flour. Remove and set aside. Blend the remaining 2 cups of the shredded coconut to coconut butter and set aside. In a food processor, place the coconut nectar, sea salt, vanilla, almond butter, and strawberries. Process until smooth. Add the coconut flour and process until well combined. Spread out onto a piece of tinfoil in a rectangle 1/2 inch thick, and place in the fridge for about an hour to firm up.
Once firm, cut into hearts with a small cookie cutter (or cut into squares). Store in the refrigerator.

Raw Almond Joy Fudge
makes about 16 squares

3 cups dried, finely shredded coconut
 1/2 cup coconut nectar
1/2 tsp sea salt
1 Tbsp pure vanilla extract
4 Tbsp raw macadamia butter or raw almond butter
6 Tbsp filtered water
1/2 cup finely shredded dried coconut
1 cup chopped raw chocolate
1 1/2 cups chopped raw almonds

 In a blender, grind one cup of the shredded coconut to flour. Remove and set aside. Blend the remaining 2 cups of the shredded coconut to coconut butter and set aside. In a food processor, place the coconut nectar, sea salt, vanilla, almond butter, and water. Process until smooth. Add the coconut flour and process until well combined. Place in a bowl and stir in 1/2 cup coconut, raw chocolate and raw almonds. Spread out onto a piece of tinfoil in a rectangle 1/2 inch thick, and place in the refrigerator for about an hour to firm up. Once firm, cut into 16 squares and enjoy.

Brownies and Bars

I know when it comes to bars, brownies are king to most people, but I enjoy things such as filled bars with a crust and chocolate like Nanaimo bars just as much. So I have included my favorites for both, everything from beet strawberry love brownies to grasshopper (chocolate mint) bars.

Raw Banana Peanut Butter Brownies
Makes 12

Brownies:
2 cups raw almond meal
1 cup sprouted oat flour (or additional almonds)
2 cups dried shredded unsweetened coconut
1/4 tsp sea salt
3/4 cup raw cacao powder
1 tsp pure vanilla extract
12 medjool dates, pitted
3 Tbsp raw coconut nectar
4 small organic bananas
1/2 cup raw peanut butter, warmed until more liquidy

2 bananas, sliced

Frosting:
1/4 cup raw peanut butter, warmed until more liquid-like
1/4 cup raw cacao powder
1/4 cup plus 2 Tbsp raw coconut or raw agave nectar (or more if needed)
Decoration:
1/4 cup raw peanut butter

To make brownies, Combine almond meal, sprouted oat flour, coconut, sea salt
and cacao powder in a high powered blender and grind to fine flour. In a food
processor, combine the vanilla, dates, coconut nectar, and bananas and process
until smooth. Add the flour and process until well blended. Spread out onto a teflex
lined dehydrator sheet and make lines of the 1/2 cup peanut butter over the batter.
Drag a knife through them to create marbling (or you can just drop random blobs
of peanut butter over the batter instead of lines if you do not wish to go through the
trouble because it will be covered). Dry in the dehydrator at 115 degrees for about
12 hours. Flip over and continue to dry a few hours more until dry but still a little
moist in the center.
Top the brownies with the banana slices, making sure the whole thing is covered.
To make the frosting, whisk together all ingredients until smooth and a frosting
consistency (adding more cacao powder if too thin, or more coconut nectar if too

thick). Spread the frosting over the brownies. Place the 1/4 cup frosting for decoration in a pastry bag (or a Ziplock bag with the end cut off), and make lines over the frosting on the brownies. Place in the freezer to set the frosting for about 30 minutes (making it easier to slice), and slice into 12 brownies. Enjoy.

Raw Tiramisu Brownies
Makes 12

Brownies:
1 1/2 cups raw almond meal (flour)
2 cups sprouted oat flour (or additional almond meal)
2 cups dried shredded unsweetened coconut
1/4 tsp sea salt
1 tsp pure vanilla extract
12 medjool dates, pitted
1/3 cup coconut water
1/3 cup raw coconut nectar
2 cups fresh coconut meat
2 tsp coffee extract

1/2 cup raw cacao powder
Coffee Cream:
1/2 cup raw cashew pieces (preferably soaked overnight)
2 Tbsp coconut water
1/2 cups fresh young coconut meat (or additional soaked cashews if not available)
2 Tbsp raw coconut nectar, raw agave nectar or raw honey
1/8 tsp sea salt
1 teaspoon pure vanilla extract
1 tsp coffee extract
2 Tbsp raw coconut oil (warmed to liquid)

Grated raw chocolate

To make brownies, Combine almond meal, sprouted oat flour, coconut, and sea salt in a high powered blender and grind to fine flour. In a food processor, combine the vanilla, dates, coconut nectar, coconut water, coconut meat, and coffee extract Process until smooth. Add the flour and process until well blended. Divide the mixture in two and return half to the food processor. Place the other half in a bowl and set aside. Add the cacao powder to the half in the food processor and process until well combined. Spread the cacao batter out onto a teflex lined dehydrator sheet into a 1/2 inch thick rectangle. Then spread the vanilla coffee batter over it. Dry in the dehydrator* at 115 degrees for about 12 hours. Flip over and continue to dry a few hours more until dry but still a little moist in the center.

For the coffee cream, combine all ingredients except the coconut oil in the food processor and process until smooth. With the motor running, add the coconut oil and process a minute longer. Place in the freezer in a bowl for about 30-45 minutes until it is the consistency of whipped cream, then place in a pastry bag and pipe over the brownies. Sprinkle with the raw chopped chocolate and cut into 12 bars. Store in the refrigerator.

*If you do not own a dehydrator and keeping them raw is not a concern, you can bake them in the oven at the lowest temp, but check them a lot sooner, as in a couple hours, since they cook a lot faster than if dehydrated and you do not want them to be too dry.

Raw Minty Brownie Bites

Makes 9-12

2 1/2 cups raw almond meal*
2 1/2 cups dried shredded unsweetened coconut
1 cup sprouted buckwheat flour or additional coconut
1/4 tsp sea salt
1 tsp pure vanilla extract
1 tsp peppermint extract
1/2 cup raw coconut nectar
a few large handfuls organic spinach
1/4 cup raw cacao powder

mint cream:
1/2 cup raw cashew pieces (preferably soaked overnight)
2 Tbsp coconut water
1/2 cups fresh young coconut meat (or additional soaked cashews if not available)
2 Tbsp raw coconut nectar, raw agave nectar or raw honey
1/8 tsp sea salt
1 teaspoon pure vanilla extract
1/2 tsp peppermint extract
1 small handful spinach
2 Tbsp raw coconut oil (warmed to liquid)

Fudge glaze:
1/3 cup raw cacao powder
1/3 cup raw coconut nectar or raw agave nectar
1 Tbsp raw coconut oil, warmed to liquid
1 tsp pure vanilla extract
a pinch sea salt

For the cake, combine the almond meal, coconut, buckwheat flour, and sea salt in the food processor, and process until finely ground like flour. Add vanilla, coconut nectar, peppermint extract, and spinach. Process until smooth and evenly blended. Remove half the batter from the food processor and set aside. To the remaining half in the processor, add the 1/4 cup cacao powder and process until blended. Place the chocolate dough on a lined dehydrator sheet, and use a rolling pin and your hands to create an even square about 3/4 inch thick. Roll the green dough out in the same fashion and place on top of the chocolate, pressing down so they stick together into one large piece. Dehydrate at 115 for about 8 hours, until dried but still moist in the center.

For the mint cream, combine all ingredients except the coconut oil in the food processor and process until smooth. With the motor running, add the coconut oil and process a minute longer. Spread the mixture over the brownies, and place in the freezer to set for about an hour.

For the fudge glaze, whisk together all ingredients in a bowl until smooth (adding more coconut oil if too thick, and more cacao if too thin) and a spreadable fudgy frosting consistency. Spread over the mint cream layer on the brownies, and place in the freezer for about 5 minutes. Cut into small 2x2 inch squares.

*I use soaked, dried almonds which have been ground in the food processor to flour, but you can also use almond pulp that has been dehydrated.

Raw Strawberry Beet Love Brownies
Makes 12

Brownies:
1 1/2 cups raw almond meal
2 cups sprouted oat flour (or additional almonds)
2 cups dried shredded unsweetened coconut
1/4 tsp sea salt
1 tsp pure vanilla extract
12 medjool dates, pitted
3 Tbsp raw coconut nectar
1 cup organic beets, shredded
2 cups organic strawberries
1/2 cup raw cacao powder

Strawberry cream:
1/2 cup raw cashew pieces (preferably soaked overnight)
2 Tbsp coconut water
1/2 cups fresh young coconut meat (or additional soaked cashews if not available)
2 Tbsp raw coconut nectar, raw agave nectar or raw honey
1/8 tsp sea salt
1 teaspoon pure vanilla extract

4 organic strawberries
2 Tbsp raw coconut oil (warmed to liquid)

Fudge glaze:
1/3 cup raw cacao powder
1/3 cup raw coconut nectar or raw agave nectar
1 Tbsp raw coconut oil, warmed to liquid
1 tsp pure vanilla extract
a pinch sea salt

To make brownies, Combine almond meal, sprouted oat flour, coconut, and sea salt in a high powered blender and grind to fine flour. In a food processor, combine the vanilla, dates, coconut nectar, beets, and strawberries. Process until smooth. Add the flour and process until well blended. Divide the mixture in two and return half to the food processor. Place the other half in a bowl and set aside. Add the cacao powder to the half in the food processor and process until well combined. Spread the cacao batter out onto a teflex lined dehydrator sheet into a 1/2 inch thick rectangle. Then spread the strawberry beet batter over it. Dry in the dehydrator* at 115 degrees for about 12 hours. Flip over and continue to dry a few hours more until dry but still a little moist in the center.

For the strawberry cream, combine all ingredients except the coconut oil in the food processor and process until smooth. With the motor running, add the coconut oil and process a minute longer. Spread the mixture over the brownies, and place in the freezer to set for about an hour.

For the fudge glaze, whisk together all ingredients in a bowl until smooth (adding more coconut oil if too thick, and more cacao if too thin) and a spreadable fudgy frosting consistency. Spread over the mint cream layer on the brownies, and place in the freezer for about 5 minutes. Cut into small 2x2 inch squares.

Raw Strawberry Lemon Cake Bars
Makes 9

2 1/2 cups raw almond meal*
2 1/2 cups dried shredded unsweetened coconut
1 cup sprouted buckwheat flour or additional coconut
1/4 tsp sea salt
1 tsp pure vanilla extract
2 Tbsp lemon juice
2 Tbsp lemon zest
1/2 cup raw coconut nectar
1/2 cup fresh organic strawberries

strawberry and lemon cream:
2 cups raw cashew pieces (preferably soaked overnight)
1/2 cup lemon juice
2Tbsp organic lemon zest
2 cups fresh young coconut meat (or additional soaked cashews if not available)
1/2 cup raw coconut nectar, raw agave nectar or raw honey
1/2 tsp sea salt
1 Tbsp pure vanilla extract
1/2 cup raw coconut oil (warmed to liquid)

1/2 cup fresh organic strawberries

For the cake, combine the almond meal, coconut, buckwheat flour, and sea salt in
the food processor, and process until finely ground like flour. Add vanilla, coconut
nectar, lemon juice and zest. Process until smooth and evenly blended. Remove
half the batter from the food processor and set aside. To the remaining half in the
processor, add the 1/2 cup strawberries and process until blended. Place the lemon
dough on a lined dehydrator sheet, and spread out to an even square about 3/4 inch
thick. Place the strawberry dough on top of the lemon, and spread it to the sides to
create 2 even layers. Dehydrate at 115 for about 8 hours, until dried but still moist
in the center.
For the strawberry and lemon creams, combine all ingredients except the coconut
oil and strawberries in the food processor and process until smooth. With the motor

running, add the coconut oil and process a minute longer. Remove half of the cream from the food processor and set aside in a bowl. Add the strawberries to the remaining cream and process until smooth and well blended. Pour into another bowl, and place in the freezer for about 45 minutes or until it is frosting consistency. Once chilled, spread the strawberry cream over the bars, then place the lemon cream in a pastry bag and pipe over the strawberry cream. Cut into 9 bars.

Raw Grasshopper Bars (chocolate mint bars)
Makes 16 bars

Crust:
2 cups raw walnuts
2 cup finely shredded dried coconut
1 1/2 cup buckwheat, sprouted and dehydrated (or additional coconut)
1/2 tsp sea salt
1/4 cup plus 2 Tbsp raw cacao powder
24 soft medjool dates, pitted (if not soft, soak them until they are and drain them)

Cream:
2 cups ripe avocado, diced
1/3 cup raw coconut nectar or raw agave nectar
1/4 tsp sea salt
seeds of one vanilla bean, or 1 Tbsp pure vanilla extract
1 tsp mint extract
a handful of spinach
1/2 cup raw coconut butter
Chocolate glaze:
1/2 cup raw cacao powder
1/2 cup raw coconut oil
1/4 cup raw coconut nectar or raw agave nectar
a pinch of sea salt

For the crust, combine walnuts, coconut, buckwheat, sea salt, cacao powder, and dates in the food processor and process until fine crumbs and starting to hold together when squeezed. Press the mixture into a foil lined 9 inch square pan, and set aside in the refrigerator. To make the cream, combine all ingredients but the coconut butter in a food processor and process until smooth. With the motor running, add the coconut butter and process a minute more. Pour the cream over the crust and place in the freezer until firmed up, about an hour. Meanwhile, to make the chocolate glaze, whisk together all ingredients until smooth, and then pour enough of the chocolate over the cream to make a thin layer (you may not need it all). Place in the freezer just until set, about 5 minutes, then cut into squares. They cut easier if you warm the knife in warm water, wipe it dry then cut a slice (to soften chocolate).

Raw Banana Coconut Nanaimo Bars
Makes 16 bars

Crust:
2 cups raw walnuts
2 cup finely shredded dried coconut
1 1/2 cup buckwheat, sprouted and dehydrated (or additional coconut)
1/2 tsp sea salt
1/4 cup plus 2 Tbsp raw cacao powder
24 soft medjool dates, pitted (if not soft, soak them until they are and drain them)

2 organic bananas, sliced

Cream:
1 cup raw cashews, soaked 4 hours and drained
1 cup young coconut meat (or additional cashews if unavailable)
1/4 cup coconut water
3 Tbsp raw coconut nectar or agave nectar
1/4 tsp sea salt
seeds of one vanilla bean, or 1 Tbsp pure vanilla extract
1 Tbsp coconut butter
1/4 cup raw coconut oil, warmed to liquid

Chocolate glaze:
1/2 cup raw cacao powder
1/2 cup raw coconut oil
1/4 cup raw coconut nectar or raw agave nectar
a pinch of sea salt

For the crust, combine walnuts, coconut, buckwheat, sea salt, cacao powder, and dates in the food processor and process until fine crumbs and starting to hold together when squeezed. Press the mixture into a foil lined 9 inch square pan. Top with the banana slices, and set aside in the refrigerator.
To make the cream, combine all ingredients but the coconut butter and oil in a food processor and process until smooth. With the motor running, add the coconut butter and oil, and process a minute more. Pour the cream over the bananas in the crust and place in the freezer until firmed up, about an hour.
Meanwhile, to make the chocolate glaze, whisk together all ingredients until smooth, then pour enough of the chocolate over the cream to make a thin layer (you may not need it all). Place in the freezer just until set, about 5 minutes, then

cut into squares. They cut easier if you warm the knife in warm water, wipe it dry then cut a slice (to soften chocolate).

Raw Pumpkin Caramel Bars

Makes 9-12

Crust:

1 1/2 cups raw walnuts, soaked and dried
1 1/2 cups raw pecans, soaked and dried
16 soft medjool dates, pitted and chopped
1 tsp cinnamon
1/2 tsp sea salt

Filling:
1 cup raw cashews (preferably soaked 6 hours)
1/2 cup fresh young coconut meat (or additional cashews if not available)
1/4 cup coconut water (or filtered water)
1 Tbsp lemon juice
1/4 cup raw agave nectar or raw honey
1 inch piece fresh ginger, chopped
1/2 Tbsp ground cinnamon
1 tsp cardamom
1/4 tsp nutmeg
1/4 teaspoon sea salt
1/2 Tbsp pure vanilla extract and seeds from half a vanilla bean (other half reserved for topping)
1 cup chopped raw organic squash or pumpkin*
1/3 cup coconut oil (warmed to liquid)

Caramel:
10 medjool dates
2 Tbsp raw coconut butter or macadamia butter (raw almond butter will also work)
3 Tbsp raw agave nectar or honey
1 tsp maple extract
1 Tbsp pure vanilla extract
1 Tbsp coconut oil
1/4 tsp fleur de sel
1/4 cup filtered water (or more if too thick, add an additional Tbsp at a time)

Cream :
1 1/2 cup raw cashew pieces (preferably soaked overnight)
1/2 cup coconut water
2 cups fresh young coconut meat (or additional soaked cashews if not available)
1/4 cup plus 2 tablespoons raw agave nectar or raw honey
2 teaspoons vanilla and seeds of half a vanilla bean (the other half of the one you

used for the filling)
1/2 cup coconut oil (warmed to liquid)

Line a 9 inch square pan with foil and lightly coat with coconut oil. To prepare the crust, process walnuts, pecans, cinnamon, and sea salt in a food processor until the nuts are fine crumbs, then add the dates and process until the mixture holds together when squeezed between your fingers. Firmly press crust into the bottom of the prepared pan, and set aside in the freezer.

To make the filling, drain the cashews and combine them with coconut water, lemon juice, agave nectar, ginger, spices, sea salt, vanilla, and squash in a food processor and blend until smooth and creamy. Slowly add the oil to the food processor with the motor running and let process until well blended. Remove the filling from the food processor, and press through a fine mesh strainer (if a smoother result is desired, but you can skip this step if you don't mind). Pour over the prepared crust and place in the freezer a couple hours until set.

Meanwhile, to make caramel, combine all ingredients in the food processor and process until smooth (if too thick add a little more water 1 Tbsp at a time). Press the caramel mixture through a fine mesh strainer to get rid of any date bits (optional, but makes for a prettier caramel). Smooth over the cheesecake layer of filling and place in the freezer to set.

Meanwhile, to make the topping, combine all ingredients but the coconut oil in the food processor, and process until smooth. Add the coconut oil with the motor running and process about a minute more. Place in a bowl and put in the freezer to set until frosting consistency, about an hour.

Place the topping in a pastry bag and pipe over the top of the caramel filling (or if you don't want to deal with that and don't care if it looks as pretty, spread it over). Cut into 12 bars or 9 if you are like me.

Fruit Desserts

There is nothing like a perfectly ripe peach turned into a crumble, accompanied by ice cream or cream. Or maybe sweet apples, used the same way in the winter. Fruit crumble is a favorite of mine, but I also enjoy things like trifles using fruit, so you will find those in this chapter as well.

Raw Lavender Peach Trifle
Serves 2

1 1/2 cups almonds
1 1/4 cups dried shredded unsweetened coconut
1/4 tsp sea salt
3 Tbsp agave nectar or honey
1 tsp pure vanilla extract

Cream:
1/2 cup raw cashew pieces (preferably soaked overnight)
1/4 cup coconut water
1/4 cup plus 2 Tbsp fresh young coconut meat* (or additional soaked cashews if not available)
1 tablespoons agave nectar or maple syrup
1/2 teaspoon pure vanilla extract
2 Tbsp coconut oil (warmed to liquid)

Sauce and Peaches:
2 tsp dried lavender
1 large organic peach, sliced
1 Tbsp honey
1 tsp pure vanilla extract

dried lavender for topping

To make the cake, combine the almonds, coconut, and sea salt in a food processor and process until finely ground. Add the agave nectar and vanilla. Process until holding together. Press into a one inch tall square, and refrigerate until firm.
To make the cream, drain cashews and blend all ingredients until smooth in a food processor, and set in the freezer about 30 minutes until a whipped cream consistency.
Puree half the peach in the food processor with lavender, honey, and vanilla until smooth. Fold half the sauce into 2/3 of the cream mixture reserving the other 1/3 for topping. Stir the remaining puree into the remaining peach slices.
Cut the cake into 1 inch cubes. To assemble trifle, spoon 1/2 the lavender cream mixture into the bottom of a medium sized bowl, and top with half the peach slices. Top with the cake, then the rest of the lavender cream mixture then the remaining peach slices. Top with the plain cream, and top with some dried lavender for garnish. Serve.

Raw Peach Crumble Timbale
makes 2

Crumble:
1 cup pecans
4 soft pitted dates
1/8 tsp sea salt or to taste

1/2 tsp cinnamon
1 Tbsp maple syrup
1/2 cup coursely chopped pecans

Peaches:
4 ripe organic medium peaches, sliced
2 Tbsp maple syrup
1 tsp pure vanilla extract
1/2 tsp cinnamon
your favorite raw ice cream

In a food processor, combine 1 cup pecans, dates and sea salt and process until finely ground. Place in a bowl and mix in maple syrup and chopped pecans with hands until it holds together a little when squeezed. Set aside.
In a large bowl, combine peaches, maple syrup, vanilla and cinnamon, and mix well. Let sit for at least 30 minutes.
To assemble, place a 4 inch round ring mold on each of two plates (or I used the top part of my 4 inch springform pan. You can also use a 4 inch wide can with the bottom cut out.) place 1/2 of the peach mixture (dividing between the two molds) into the bottom of the molds, arranging the peaches so they are flat and pretty. Top with half the crumble mixture, then the other half of the peach mixture then the remaining crumble mixture. Carefully remove the molds, and serve with ice cream

Raw Caramel Apple Crumble Timbale
Makes 2

Crumble:
1 cup pecans
1 cup finely shredded dried coconut
8 soft pitted dates
1/8 tsp sea salt or to taste
1/2 tsp cinnamon
1 Tbsp agave nectar or honey
3/4 cup coursely chopped pecans

Apples:
3 large organic Honeycrisp (or other tart sweet apples), sliced and slices halved
2 Tbsp agave nectar or honey
12 medjool dates, pitted
1 tsp pure vanilla extract
2 tsp cinnamon
1/2 tsp nutmeg
juice of one lemon
a pinch of sea salt

Caramel:
10 medjool dates, pitted
1 Tbsp almond butter
2 Tbsp agave nectar or honey
1/4 tsp sea salt
1 Tbsp coconut oil
1 tsp pure vanilla extract
2 Tbsp water

Raw Apple Cinnamon Ice Cream:
(recipe follows)

In a food processor, combine 1 cup pecans, coconut, dates and sea salt and process until finely ground. Place in a bowl and mix in agave nectar and chopped pecans with hands until it holds together a little when squeezed. Set aside.

Place one of the apples in a food processor with the agave nectar, cinnamon, nutmeg, lemon juice, vanilla and sea salt and process until almost smooth. In a large bowl, combine puree, and apple slices, and mix well. Spread out on a dehydrator tray and dry for 2 hours, or until slightly softened. Scrape mixture into a bowl.

To make caramel, combine all ingredients in a food processor until smooth.

To assemble, place a 4 inch round ring mold on each of two plates, or I used the top part of my 4 inch springform pan. You can also use a 4 inch wide can with the bottom cut out. Place 1/3 of the nut mixture into the bottom of each (dividing between the two). Then, 1/2 of the apple mixture (dividing between the two molds), arranging the apples so they are flat and pretty. Drizzle each with a little of the caramel. Top with half the remaining crumble mixture, then the other half of the apple mixture then a little more caramel, then the remaining crumble mixture. Carefully remove the molds, drizzle with a little more caramel, and serve with Raw Apple Cinnamon ice cream.

Raw Apple Cinnamon Ice Cream
Makes about 3 cups

1 large organic Honeycrisp apple, sliced (or other flavorful apple)
1 cup raw cashews, soaked for at least 2 hours and drained
1 cup young coconut meat, chopped
1/2 cup young coconut water
1/4 cup agave nectar or honey
a large pinch of sea salt
seeds of one vanilla bean
2 tsp ground Vietnamese cinnamon
1 tsp maple extract
1/4 cup coconut oil, warmed to liquid

In a food processor, combine the apple, cashews, coconut, coconut water, agave nectar, sea salt, cinnamon, and maple extract, and process until smooth. With the processor running, pour in the coconut oil and process until well incorporated, about a minute. Pour the mixture into an ice cream maker and process according to directions. Once processed, pour into a freezer safe container with a lid, and let harden until scoopable consistency, about 4 hours or overnight.

Citrus Carpaccio with Grapefruit Lavender Ice Cream, Pistachio Crumble, and Lavender Syrup

Serves 2

Syrup:
2 Tbsp raw agave nectar or raw honey
2 Tbsp water
2 tsp dried lavender flowers
1 tsp pure vanilla extract

Crumble:
1/4 cup raw pistachios, shelled
1/4 cup large flake coconut
1 Tbsp agave nectar
a large pinch sea salt

2 pink grapefruits (such as Rio Stars), Peeled, and thinly sliced horizintally
2 oranges, peeled and thinly sliced horizontally
1/4 cup pomegranate seeds

Raw Grapefruit Lavender Ice Cream (recipe follows)

For the syrup, combine all ingredients together in a small bowl, and stir to dissolve agave nectar. Let sit for at least a few hours.

For the crumble, combine the pistachios, coconut, agave nectar, and sea salt in the blender and pulse until coarsely chopped and sticking together a bit.

On each of 2 plates, place the grapefruit and orange slices decoratively, and scatter some pomegranate seeds. Place a scoop of the ice cream, then spoon some of the crumble around it. Drizzle the syrup over the citrus. Enjoy.

Raw Pink Grapefruit Lavender Ice Cream
Makes about 4 cups

1 cup grapefruit juice
3 Tbsp grapefruit zest
2 cups raw cashews, soaked overnight and drained
2 cups young coconut meat, chopped
1/2 cup raw agave nectar or raw honey
seeds of one vanilla bean
a pinch of sea salt
1/2 cup coconut oil, warmed to liquid
3 Tbsp dried lavender

Add grapefruit juice to a food processor, along with zest, cashews, coconut meat, agave nectar, vanilla, and sea salt. Process until smooth, then with the processor running, add the coconut oil slowly and process until well incorporated, about a minute. Pour the mixture through a fine mesh strainer and press through until you have removed any coconut bits (you can skip this step, but it makes for a smoother ice cream). Stir in lavender, then pour the strained mixture into an ice cream maker and process according to directions. Remove from ice cream maker, and pour into a freezer safe container. Let chill in the freezer for a few hours until a little more firm before scooping.

Raw Tropical Fruit "Lasagna"
Serves 2

Strawberry Sauce:
1/2 cup fresh organic strawberries
3 soft, pitted medjool dates
1 tsp pure vanilla extract

Banana Coconut Cream:
1 cup fresh young Thai coconut (or 3/4 cup soaked raw cashews drained if coconut unavailable)
2 medium ripe organic bananas
2 Tbsp raw coconut nectar
1/4 cup plus 2 tbsp coconut butter, warmed to liquid
1 tsp pure vanilla extract

For assembly:
4 thin slices of organic mango (4x4 inch squares)
2 thin slices fresh organic pineapple (4x8 inch rectangles)
10 fresh organic strawberries sliced

For the strawberry sauce, combine all ingredients in the food processor and process until smooth. Set aside in the refrigerator. For the banana cream, in a high speed blender, combine all ingredients and process until smooth. Place in the refrigerator to set up to the consistency of heavy cream (about an hour).
When ready to assemble, spoon a bit of the strawberry sauce onto a serving plate. Lay out one of the pineapple slices, and top with 1/3 of the banana cream. Top with some of the sliced strawberries, then two mango slices (so they form a rectangle and fit with the rest of the lasagna evenly on the sides). Top them with half the remaining banana cream, then more strawberry slices. Top with 2 more mango slices, the rest of the cream, more strawberries, then the last pineapple slice. Spoon the strawberry sauce over and top with more berries. Serve.

Raw Red Velvet Raspberry Chocolate Crepes
Makes Two Servings

Raw Crepes:
1 ripe organic banana
6 oz organic raspberries
1 Tbsp lemon juice
1 tsp agave nectar or honey

Cream:
3/4 cup raw cashew pieces (preferably soaked overnight)
1/2 cup coconut water
3/4 cup fresh young coconut meat* (or additional soaked cashews if not available)
2 tablespoons agave nectar or honey
1 teaspoon pure vanilla extract and seeds of half a vanilla bean
3 Tbsp raw cocoa powder
1/4 cup coconut oil (warmed to liquid)

Fruit:
1 cup organic raspberries, divided
1 tsp lemon juice
1 Tbsp agave nectar or honey

Chocolate Sauce:
2 Tbsp raw cocoa powder
2 Tbsp agave nectar or honey
2 tsp coconut oil
1 tsp pure vanilla extract

To make crepes, combine all ingredients in a food processor and process until blended. Pour into 4 circles on a teflex lined dehydrator sheet, and spread thin. Dehydrate for about 8 hours or until no longer wet and tacky, but still pliable. Remove from dehydrator and set aside.
To make cream, drain cashews and blend all ingredients until smooth in a food processor, and set in the freezer about 30 minutes until a frosting consistency. Meanwhile, to make the raspberry sauce, puree 1 cup raspberries with lemon juice and agave nectar until smooth and set aside.

Fold the remaining 1/2 cup raspberries into the chocolate cream.

To make the chocolate sauce, whisk together the cocoa powder, agave nectar, coconut oil and vanilla (if too thick add a little more agave nectar, if too thin add a little more cocoa powder).

To assemble, place a crepe on your work surface then top with 1/4 of the cream filling. Roll it up, and place on a serving plate. Repeat with another crepe, and place on the same plate. Repeat with the other two and place on another plate. Drizzle the crepes on each plate with the raspberry sauce, and then the chocolate sauce. Serve

Ingredients and Tools:

Flours:

Almond Flour: To make almond flour, grind sprouted (soaked and dehydrated) almonds to a fine consistency in a high speed blender (but not too long or it will become nut butter). Store in the refrigerator.

Coconut Flour: To make coconut flour, take 3 cups of finely shredded dried coconut and blend until fine flour in a high speed blender (but not too long or it will become nut butter). Store in the refrigerator.

Sprouted Oat Flour: I use sprouted oat flour in place of flour in a few recipes, because I always have sprouted oats on hand. To make it, simply soak raw oat groats for 8 hours, then drain well. Spread out onto a dehydrator sheet and dehydrate until dry (about 24 hours). Place in a high speed blender and grind to flour. Store in the refrigerator.

Flavorings:

Vanilla: I buy whole vanilla beans to use in recipes because I believe they have the best flavor, but if you do not have access to them, feel free to use organic pure vanilla extract.

Essential Oils: Sometimes in my recipes that call for lavender or citrus I use essential oil. However you cannot just use any kind it has to be ok for consumption. Du Terra essential oils are perfect for my recipes and can be ordered on their site. I use their lavender, orange and lemon oils.

Lavender: I use dried lavender flowers in many of my recipes, and they can be bought at most health food stores in the bulk section. Just be sure they are food grade organic.

Sweeteners:

Coconut nectar: I often use coconut nectar in my recipes, as I feel it is one of the better raw liquid sweeteners. It is low glycemic and made from the sap of flowers from the coconut tree. It can be found at many raw suppliers online or in health food stores.

Raw Agave Nectar: I tend not to use as much raw agave nectar now as I used to because there is a lot of controversy around the use of it. If you cannot find coconut nectar or prefer to use agave nectar, you are welcome to.

Maple Syrup: Technically maple syrup is not raw, but it is a wonderful sweetener and contains minerals that can be beneficial.

Raw Honey: Although not vegan, honey is a wonderful liquid sweetener, and it works great in raw recipes.

Stevia: If you are diabetic or trying to stay away from sugar, stevia is a great option as it will not affect your blood sugar levels.

Dates: I use dates when I can to sweeten, because they are about the most natural sweetener you can find. I use them in crusts and to make raw caramel because of their sticky texture. I use medjool dates, which still have the pits when I buy them, because I find that they are softer than the pitted. You can use other soft dates if you like. If the dates you bought are not soft, soak them in filtered water and drain well before using in recipes.

Nuts and Seeds:

For the nuts in my recipes, I use raw nuts and always soak them. Soaking makes the nuts easier to digest. Some nuts need a longer time to soak, because they are larger or harder. Almonds will need to soak 8 hours, while cashews, pecans, walnuts, pistachios, macadamias, and hazelnuts need about 4 hours. If the recipe calls for them to be soft, such as cashews in a cheesecake filling, they are ready to use after soaking. But if the nuts need to be crunchy such as in a crust, dehydrate them for about 24 hours until dried.

Buckwheat: I often use sprouted, dehydrated buckwheat groats in my crusts because they give it a nice crunch and cut down on the nuts. To make them, simply soak the raw buckwheat groats for 30 minutes in filtered water, then rinse and drain well. Spread out on a dehydrator sheet and dehydrate until dry, about 24 hours. Buckwheat is gluten-free.

Peanut Butter: I make my own raw peanut butter from jungle peanuts, but if you are not strictly raw you can feel free to use roasted peanut butter as long as it is unsweetened (such as Maranatha brand).

Almond Butter: Almond butter is easily made at home if you have a high speed blender, but if you do not, you can buy raw in most health food stores or online.

Coconut:

Coconut Oil: I use a lot of coconut oil in my recipes involving creamy elements because it adds richness and helps them to set up properly when chilled. Also, I believe that healthy oil such as coconut is beneficial to your body and is needed in order to absorb nutrients. You always want to buy raw unrefined virgin coconut oil. Since it is solid at room temperature it will need to be warmed for use in recipes. I simply place mine in the dehydrator in a glass measuring cup until it is melted.

Coconut butter: Not to be confused with coconut oil, it is the whole flesh of coconut. I use a lot of coconut butter in my recipes because it has a wonderful sweetness and is so easy to make at home. To do so, in a high speed blender, add 3 cups finely shredded dried coconut and blend at high speed using the tamper to press it into the blades until it is smooth and creamy. This will take about 1 minute. Pour into a jar and enjoy. You can store at room temperature, and it will become solid but it will need to be warmed for use in recipes. I simply place mine in the dehydrator in a glass measuring cup (or in the glass jar I am storing it in if it fits) until it is melted.

Young coconut meat: I use a lot of fresh young coconut meat in my recipes because it is creamy and sweet. Too open you need a cleaver. Lay the coconut on its side, holding it firmly closer to the bottom, and bring the knife down near the top a few inches down from the pointed part. You should break through to the center where the water is. Set the coconut on its base so the water doesn't run out, then pour the water into a container (don't throw it away, it is delicious). Finish cutting the top off going in a circle around the top. Scoop the meat out from the coconut with a sturdy metal spoon (I use a large eating spoon).

Cacao:

I do not have access to raw cacao butter at a price that I can afford, so when I make my chocolate I use coconut oil and raw cacao. If you have access to it, feel free to use it! Chocolate made with coconut oil melts easier at room temperature. This is the recipe I use for raw chocolate when I make chocolate chunks in ice cream, cookies, or for garnish:

Raw Chocolate Chunks:

½ cup raw cacao powder
½ cup raw coconut oil, warmed to liquid
¼ cup raw coconut nectar or maple syrup
A pinch of sea salt

Whisk all ingredients together until smooth and well blended. Pour into molds, or out onto a sheet of foil and place in the fridge to harden. Chop into chunks.
I believe that raw cacao has more health benefits than regular cocoa powder, but if you cannot find raw cacao powder, you can use unsweetened natural organic cocoa powder. I buy my raw cacao online at Vitacost.

Tools:

Dehydrator: I use a dehydrator for many of my recipes to get food to the proper "cooked" or "baked" consistency but not destroy the enzymes and nutrients. They are handy to have if you are serious about a raw food diet. I use a 5 tray Excalibur dehydrator for my recipes, but I used to have a 4 tray and it worked fine also. Use what you can afford. Most dehydrators will work for my recipes, although you may have a hard time with the round ones with a hole in the middle. I recommend the square type with trays that slide in from the front. If you look online you will find that you can purchase them on sale and they are not as expensive as you may think. If you are not ready to buy a dehydrator and do not mind if your food is raw, you can use your oven at a low temperature for the recipes, but keep in mind it takes a lot less time to cook.

Food Processor: I use a Cuisinart 9 cup food processor for my recipes, and it has been very sturdy, so I would definitely recommend it. If you do not have a high powder food processor, keep in mind that you may have bits left in your batter or cream, so you may need to use a fine meshed strainer (which I sometimes do anyway, since coconut tends to leave bits).

Blender: I use a Vitamix blender for my recipes, because a powerful blender is needed when making things such as nut butters or to get your cream very smooth. However a regular blender may work if you have a tamper to push the food down into the blades so that it does not stick to the sides.

Index

125 Raw Pumpkin Caramel Bars

26 Raw Samoa Cheesecake

Carrot:

30 Raw Ginger Carrot Dream Cakes

80 Raw Sunshine Ice Cream

42 The Ultimate Raw Carrot Cake

Chipotle peppers:

89 Raw Chipotle Caramel Dark Chocolates

21 Raw Mexican Chocolate Turtle Cheesecake

Chocolate:

103 Raw Almond Joy Fudge

123 Raw Banana Coconut Nanaimo Bars

106 Raw Banana Peanut Butter Brownies

89 Raw Chipotle Caramel Dark Chocolates

147 Raw Chocolate Chunks

51 Raw Chocolate Strawberry Silk Pie

48 Raw Dark Chocolate Glazed Red Velvet Doughnuts

120 Raw Grasshopper Bars

95 Raw Key Lime Pie Truffles

91 Raw Lavender Lemon Caramel Dark Chocolates

24 Raw Lime Dark Chocolate Pistachio Cheesecake

21 Raw Mexican Chocolate Turtle Cheesecake

112 Raw Minty Brownie Bites

87 Raw Peanut Butter Caramel Cups

93 Raw Raspberry Rose Cream Truffles

76 Raw Red Velvet Chocolate Chunk Ice Cream

142 Raw Red Velvet Raspberry Chocolate Crepes

26 Raw Samoa Cheesecake

115 Raw Strawberry Beet Love Brownies

109 Raw Tiramisu Brownies

Cinnamon:

135 Raw Apple Cinnamon Ice Cream

89 Raw Chipotle Caramel Dark Chocolates

21 Raw Mexican Chocolate Turtle Cheesecake

Coconut:

146 Coconut butter

144 Coconut Flour

103 Raw Almond Joy Fudge

123 Raw Banana Coconut Nanaimo Bars

54 Raw Banana Macadamia Coconut Dream Pie

97 Raw Coconut Rose Pistachio Macaroons

99 Raw Lavender Lemon Macaroons

16 Raw Piña Colada Cheesecake

26 Raw Samoa Cheesecake

Coffee:

109 Raw Tiramisu Brownies

Ginger:

60 Blueberry Rhubarb Ginger Crumble Tart

30 Raw Ginger Carrot Dream Cakes

78 Raw Strawberry Rhubarb Ginger Ice Cream

Grapefruit:

137 Raw Citrus Carpaccio with Grapefruit Lavender Ice Cream and Lavender Syrup

138 Raw Grapefruit Lavender Ice Cream

Jam:

13 Raw PB & J Swirl Cheesecake

Lavender:

7 Raw Blackberry Lavender Cheesecake

82 Raw Blueberry Lavender Ice Cream

137 Raw Citrus Carpaccio with Grapefruit Lavender Ice Cream and Lavender Syrup

138 Raw Grapefruit Lavender Ice Cream

91 Raw Lavender Lemon Caramel Dark Chocolates

45 Raw Lemon Lavender Doughnuts

99 Raw Lavender Lemon Macaroons

129 Raw Lavender Peach Trifle

10 Raw Pretty in Pink Birthday Cheesecake

Lemon:

67 Lemon Almond Poppy seed Ice Cream

7 Raw Blackberry Lavender Cheesecake

91 Raw Lavender Lemon Caramel Dark Chocolates

99 Raw Lavender Lemon Macaroons

66 Raw Little Lemon Tart with Lemon Almond Poppy seed Ice Cream

45 Raw Lemon Lavender Doughnuts

118 Raw Strawberry Lemon Cake Bars

Lime:

84 Raw Key Lime Pie Ice Cream

95 Raw Key Lime Pie Truffles

63 Raw Lime Avocado Tart

24 Raw Lime Dark Chocolate Pistachio Cheesecake

66 Raw Little Key Lime Tart with Strawberry Lime Ice Cream

36 Raw Spring Blossom Cake

70 Raw Strawberry Lime Ice Cream

Macadamia Nuts:

54 Raw Banana Macadamia Coconut Dream Pie

16 Raw Piña Colada Cheesecake

Mango:

36 Raw Spring Blossom Cake

80 Raw Sunshine Ice Cream

140 Raw Tropical Fruit Lasagna

Mint:

120 Raw Grasshopper Bars

112 Raw Minty Brownie Bites

Oats:

144 Sprouted Oat Flour

Orange:

137 Raw Citrus Carpaccio with Grapefruit Lavender Ice Cream and Lavender Syrup

80 Raw Sunshine Ice Cream

Peach:

129 Raw Lavender Peach Trifle

131 Raw Peach Crumble Timbale

Peanut Butter:

106 Raw Banana Peanut Butter Brownies

13 Raw PB & J Swirl Cheesecake

87 Raw Peanut Butter Caramel Cups

Pecans:

72 Raw Baklava with Saffron Ice Cream

57 Mini Raw Sweet Potato Caramel Pecan Pies

21 Raw Mexican Chocolate Turtle Cheesecake

Pineapple:

16 Raw Piña Colada Cheesecake

140 Raw Tropical Fruit Lasagna

Pistachios:

97 Raw Coconut Rose Pistachio Macaroons

24 Raw Lime Dark Chocolate Pistachio Cheesecake

Poppy seeds:

66 Raw Little Lemon Tart with Lemon Almond Poppy seed Ice Cream

67 Raw Lemon Almond Poppy seed Ice Cream

Pumpkin:

125 Raw Pumpkin Caramel Bars

Raspberries:

10 Raw Pretty In Pink Birthday Cheesecake

13 Raw PB & J Swirl Cheesecake

142 Raw Red Velvet Raspberry Chocolate Crepes

93 Raw Raspberry Rose Cream Truffles

Rhubarb:

60 Blueberry Rhubarb Ginger Crumble Tart

78 Raw Strawberry Rhubarb Ginger Ice Cream

Rose:

97 Raw Coconut Rose Pistachio Macaroons

93 Raw Raspberry Rose Cream Truffles

Saffron:

72 Raw Baklava with Saffron Ice Cream

73 Raw Saffron Ice Cream

Strawberries:

51 Raw Chocolate Strawberry Silk Pie

10 Raw Pretty In Pink Birthday Cheesecake

70 Raw Strawberry Lime Ice Cream

36 Raw Spring Blossom Cake

18 Raw Strawberries and Cream Dream Cake

101 Raw Strawberries and Cream Fudge

115 Raw Strawberry Beet Love Brownies

118 Raw Strawberry Lemon Cake Bars

78 Raw Strawberry Rhubarb Ginger Ice Cream

39 Raw Strawberry Shortcake

140 Raw Tropical Fruit Lasagna

Sweet Potatoes:

57 Mini Raw Sweet Potato Caramel Pecan Pies

31524221R00085

Printed in Great Britain
by Amazon